Praise for
Masculinities in the Making

"*Masculinities in the Making* is an important contribution to gender studies—a book that develops hegemonic masculinity theory, discusses new non-conformist sex and gender patterns, and includes an utterly scary analysis of how masculine fantasy can become global political reality. Warmly recommended!"
—Øystein Gullvåg Holter, Centre for Gender Research, University of Oslo

"In *Masculinities in the Making*, James W. Messerschmidt brings together some of his key ideas, ranging from theoretical and sociological concerns such as structure and action, to detailed analyses of wimps, genderqueers, and US presidents. The book shows the complexity of this venture and sets out a clear agenda for further and future studies of masculinities. This is another must-read for all those concerned with these questions."
—Jeff Hearn, Örebro University, Sweden; Hanken School of Economics, Finland; University of Huddersfield, UK; and author of *Men of the World*

D1004542

MASCULINITIES IN THE MAKING

From the Local to the Global

James W. Messerschmidt

ROWMAN & LITTLEFIELD
Lanham • Boulder • New York • London

Published by Rowman & Littlefield
A wholly owned subsidiary of
The Rowman & Littlefield Publishing Group, Inc.
4501 Forbes Boulevard, Suite 200, Lanham, Maryland 20706
www.rowman.com

Unit A, Whitacre Mews, 26-34 Stannary Street, London SE11 4AB,
United Kingdom

British Library Cataloguing in Publication Information Available

Library of Congress Cataloging-in-Publication Data
Messerschmidt, James W.
Masculinities in the making : from the local to the global / James W. Messerschmidt.
pages cm
Includes bibliographical references and index.
ISBN 978-1-4422-3292-1 (cloth : alk. paper) — ISBN 978-1-4422-3293-8 (pbk. : alk. paper) —
ISBN 978-1-4422-3294-5 (electronic)
1. Masculinity. 2. Men—Psychology. I. Title.
BF692.5.M47 2015
305.31—dc23
2015017467

∞ ™ The paper used in this publication meets the minimum requirements of
American National Standard for Information Sciences Permanence of Paper
for Printed Library Materials, ANSI/NISO Z39.48-1992.

Printed in the United States of America

CONTENTS

INTRODUCTION

Since the 1960s various forms of feminism have continually challenged the masculinist nature of academia by illuminating the patterns of gendered power that social theory had for centuries all but ignored. In particular, feminism secured a permanent role for sex, gender, and sexuality politics in popular culture and thereby moved analysis of sex, gender, and sexual power to the forefront of much social thought. The growth and maturation of explicit theoretical development and empirical research on masculinities followed logically from this feminist work because if sex, gender, and sexuality are conceptualized in terms of power relations, then studying not simply the powerless but also the powerful becomes necessary. As with any structure of power and inequality (such as race, class, and nation), it is essential to study the powerful, and this of course includes men, masculinities, and heterosexualities.

Masculinities in the Making aims to make a contribution to this expansion and development of research and theorizing on masculinities by bringing together several of my past studies into one volume. These studies demonstrate the complexity involved in the making of masculinities, they concentrate on what may be considered rather inconspicuous forms of masculinities (those constructed by wimps, genderqueers, and presidents), and they reveal new insight for the sociology of masculinities.

The book is divided into five chapters and an afterword. Chapter 1, "Hegemony and Beyond," is an assessment of selected scholarly articles on the concept of *hegemonic masculinity* (Connell, 1987; 1995) at local, regional, and global levels and how these works contribute to gendered knowledge. I examine how hegemonic masculinity has been appropriated differently and what this dissimilarity means for gendered knowledge construction. The chapter goes on to highlight several new scholarly directions on hegemonic masculinity, the relevance for all this work to the wider debates over the concept of hegemonic masculinity, the necessity of moving beyond simply investigations of how masculinities are embedded in gender hegemonic relations to include masculinities that fall outside such relations, and how these conclusions relate to the chapters that follow.

Chapter 2, "Masculinities as Structured Action," outlines a newly revised *structured action theory* that I have developed and published in differing forms since 1993. The bulk of the book is the application of this theory to the three major studies I have accomplished during my academic career and are reported in chapters 3, 4, and 5.

Chapter 3, "Wimps: Sam and Jerry," focuses on two white working-class teenage boys from New England—Sam and Jerry (both pseudonyms)—who were both bullied as *wimps* and thus the chapter concentrates on how this bullying victimization is related to their specific constructions of localized masculinities. In the late 1990s I did life-history interviews of teenage boys and girls to examine the construction and formation of gender and sexual practices through violent and nonviolent social action. Thirty youth (fifteen boys and fifteen girls) were interviewed and prior to each interview I obtained the informed consent of each participant. I also used a "maximum-variation" sampling procedure that provided a selection of interviewees from a wide range of home life and other background situations. The thirty life-history case studies—although not a representative sample—revealed the more elusive elements of teenage life that are often difficult to capture in quantifiable variables. Each life story deepens and augments our understanding of how eventual sex/gender/sexuality construction is related to personal life history.

The life-history method implemented in chapter 3 involved voluntary and confidential one-on-one tape-recorded "informal conversational interviews" (Patton, 1990: 280–282). These conversations were completed in two meetings of approximately three hours each. The conversations were fluid, allowing each interviewee to take the lead rather than merely to respond to topical questions. The goal was to grasp each individual's unique viewpoint and thus personal vision of the world. This interview method involved attempting to foster collaboration (rather than hierarchy) in the research process by judiciously engaging each interviewee, "working interactionally to establish the discursive bases from which the respondent can articulate his or her relevant experiences" (Holstein and Gubrium, 1995: 47).

This does not mean, however, that the conversations were unstructured. On the contrary, each conversation attempted to unearth the situational interactions and accomplishment of embodied practices in particular contexts and as related to personal life history. As such, the interviews sought detailed descriptions of practices (both what interviewees did and how they reflexively internally deliberated about particular social interactions and future actions) and accounts of structured interaction in families, peer/leisure groups, schools, and workplaces. The conversations touched on intimate and sensitive areas of personal life and relationships. Thus, the interviews reveal individual agentic trajectories through an assemblage of social structures in institutions and organizations.

The "data analysis" for this study had two stages. First, tape-recorded conversations were transcribed and second, individual case studies prepared. In chapter 3 I dissect two of the life histories and define the similarities and differences among their pathways to particular forms of masculinities. The goal is to capture embodied experience for each interviewee in his words. By comparing the two individual life stories of Sam and Jerry I establish links between the two teenage boys who construct masculinity differently. In other words, I discover the interconnections between two boys as well as the differences between them. Accordingly, life-history methodology helps to register patterns in lives that other methodologies render invisible.

Chapter 4, "Genderqueers: Jessie and Morgan," investigates two white young adults from New England—Jessie and Morgan (both pseudonyms)—who self-identify as *genderqueer*, meaning they consider oneself as *both* masculine and feminine (Jessie) or as *neither* masculine nor feminine (Morgan). In 2010 and 2011 I completed life-history interviews of fourteen genderqueer people, all of whom were assigned female at birth yet came to perceive that exclusive femininity is an incomplete description of their gender. In constructing both masculinity and femininity or neither masculinity nor femininity genderqueer people challenge the heteronormative congruence among sex, gender, and sexuality and live in a way that questions traditional sex, gender, and sexuality assumptions. However, at different stages of their life history, both Jessie and Morgan constructed different forms of localized masculinities.

For the overall study of genderqueers I chose fourteen individuals with the help of a "contact" associated with various transgender communities throughout New England. This "contact" also was hired as a research assistant who coordinated with me the selection of interviewees, which we accomplished using a "maximum-variation" sampling procedure to ensure interviewees were from a wide range of home life and other background situations. Prior to each interview I obtained the informed consent of each participant being interviewed. The fourteen life-history case studies—although not a representative sample—reveal the more elusive elements of becoming genderqueer that are often difficult to capture in quantifiable variables. Each life story deepens and augments our understanding of how eventual sex, gender, and sexuality construction is related to personal life history. And the life-history method implemented in chapter 4 is the same as that used in chapter 3.

Chapter 5, "Presidents: Bush and Obama," examines the orchestration of regional and global hegemonic masculinities through an examination of the speeches of these two most recent U.S. presidents as contrasting forms of communicative social action. In 2009 I decided to examine *all* of Bush's speeches (public addresses) that focused on Iraq from January 29, 2002, to the U.S.-led military invasion against Iraq on March 19, 2003. And most recently I have concentrated on and examined Obama's speeches that centered on Afghanistan from January 20, 2009, to December 31, 2014. For both Bush and Obama I used the method of "content analysis" (Altheide, 1996; Berg, 1998) to examine the significant recurring features of each president's speeches and I concentrated on speeches (rather than on other forms of discourse) because such public statements are highly accessible to both regional and global audiences. Initially, I carefully and thoroughly read all of the speeches delivered during the time frames above and, using an open coding assessment, I formulated *units of analysis* (Berg, 1998). For Bush, the units of analysis that emerged were first "Saddam Hussein," second "American, Iraqi, and all 'civilized' men, women, and children," and third "George W. Bush." For Obama, first the "Taliban and Al Qaida," second "American, Afghan, and citizens of the NATO alliance," and third "Barack Obama" were the units of analysis. In the subsequent examination of each president's set of speeches, I focused on how each unit was characterized and symbolized in the speeches, how each unit was related to the other units in the speeches, and whether or not there was an identifiable narrative throughout the mix of speeches. And the content analysis revealed a definite narrative throughout both presidents' sets of speeches, communicating a particular *story*, specific *characters* constituting that story, and clearly defined *relationships* among the actors.

The conclusion briefly summarizes the key findings on the three disparate groups of wimps, genderqueers, and presidents and correspondingly provides ten suggestions for prospective and subsequent scholarship on masculinities.

Masculinities in the Making then brings together three seemingly disparate case studies—wimps, genderqueers, and presidents—to examine what insight each have to offer masculinities scholars in terms of knowledge about the social construction of masculinities by wholly distinct individuals but also what the similarities amongst them might entail. The book contributes to academic work on masculinities because sociology actually reports *very little* life-history research on either wimps or genderqueers, *no* comparative research on the hegemonic masculinities of the two most recent U.S. presidents, and *no* research that compares the various types of masculinities at the local, regional, and global levels. Furthermore, this work offers a newly revised "structured action" theory that advances what may be labelled a materialist-discursive perspective on masculinities, it highlights the intersection of sex, gender, and sexuality and thus new forms of hybrid masculinities, it underlines the significance of reflexivity to masculine structured action, it examines the variations among and between hegemonic and nonhegemonic masculinities, it compares masculinities by people assigned male and female at birth, it investigates the role of embodiment and disembodiment in masculine constructions, and it scrutinizes how masculinity may not be the sole defining aspect of one's gender identity. Thus, I believe this work will reveal novel details about masculinities in the making and thus will optimistically augment our conceptualization of the various facets associated with sex, gender, and sexuality in society today.

I am forever deeply grateful to Sam, Jerry, Jessie, and Morgan for talking openly with me and sharing their lives. Without their cooperation this book would never have been written. Although I am *not* likewise grateful for the speeches by both Bush and Obama, I must acknowledge that this book could not have been written if these two U.S. presidents had not engaged in their particular forms of communicative social action. I also want to express a special thanks to Alex Lorenzu for taking time out of a very busy schedule to provide me with detailed comments on chapter 4.

The material on Bush and Obama previously was presented in various stages of development as keynote addresses at Ruhr University, Bochum, Germany, 2012; Durham University, Durham, England, 2013; University of Vienna, Vienna, Austria, 2013; Aalborg University, Aalborg, Denmark, 2014; and University of Freiburg, Germany, 2015. The material on Jessie and Morgan was previously presented as a keynote address at a conference at Palacky University, Olomouc, Czech Republic, 2014. I thank the participants at each of these events for their extremely thoughtful remarks and reflections.

I thank Sage Publications for permission to publish chapter 1 as a revised and expanded version of "Engendering Gendered Knowledge: Assessing the Academic Appropriation of *Hegemonic Masculinity*." The final, definitive version of this paper has been published in *Men and Masculinities* 15 (1) (2012): 56–76, Sage Publications, Inc., reprinted by permission of Sage Publications, Inc. Part of chapter 5 on Bush was previously published in James W. Messerschmidt, *Hegemonic Masculinities and Camouflaged Politics: Unmasking the Bush Dynasty and Its War Against Iraq*

(Boulder, CO: Paradigm Publishers, 2010), and some of the information on Sam and Jerry in chapter 3 was previously published in James W. Messerschmidt, *Gender, Heterosexuality, and Youth Violence: The Struggle for Recognition* (Lanham, MD: Rowman & Littlefield, 2012). Although some of this material may therefore be familiar to previous readers of my work, the analysis is entirely new and based on an expanded and revised structured action theory.

I also wish to extend considerable appreciation to the entire staff at Rowman & Littlefield—my favorite publisher!—but especially to Sarah Stanton (senior acquisitions editor), who has graciously and wholeheartedly supported my work over the years, and to Kathryn Knigge and Karie Simpson (assistant editors), Alden Perkins (senior production editor), and Jocquan Mooney (copyeditor).

Most of all thanks to Ulla, Erik, Jan, and Mel—the most important people in my life!

I

HEGEMONY AND BEYOND

The academic appropriation of concepts long established as salient contributions to gender theory and research recently has come under scholarly scrutiny. For example, scholars have looked at how the historical trajectory of the concept of "doing gender" (West and Zimmerman, 1987) has been assimilated into theoretical and methodological practice (Wickes and Emmison, 2007), as well as how the concept's implications might impact the construction of future gender research and theory (Jurik and Siemsen, 2009). Moreover, during the same period scholarly attention has focused on how the unceasing ambiguity and open-endedness of the concept of "intersectionality" (Crenshaw, 1991) are the secret to its chronicled success (Davis, 2008) and on what it means to actually practice "intersectionality" as a theoretical and methodological approach to inequality (Yeon Choo and Ferree, 2010).

In this opening chapter I contribute to the scholarly dissection of crucial gender concepts by assessing the recent academic appropriation of the concept of "hegemonic masculinity" (Connell, 1987; 1995) and by determining how this appropriation engenders gendered knowledge. In what follows I first briefly revisit the concept of hegemonic masculinity as reformulated by Connell and myself (2005). Following this I address specific questions regarding the growth of this knowledge by examining selected studies to illustrate how hegemonic masculinity has been appropriated differently and what this dissimilarity means for gendered knowledge construction. I then highlight several new directions found in selected publications that extend gendered knowledge on hegemonic masculinity. Finally, I discuss the relevance of my conclusions to the wider debates over the concept of hegemonic masculinity as well as how these conclusions relate to the chapters that follow.

HEGEMONIC MASCULINITY REFORMULATED

Raewyn Connell (1987; 1995) initially conceptualized *hegemonic masculinity* as the form of masculinity in a given historical and society-wide setting that structures and legitimates hierarchical gender relations between men and women, between masculinity and femininity, and among masculinities. The relational character was central to her argument, embodying a particular form of masculinity in hierarchical relation to a certain form of femininity and to nonhegemonic masculinities. Connell emphasized that hegemonic masculinity has no meaning outside its *relationship* to "emphasized femininity"—and to nonhegemonic masculinities—or to those femininities practiced in a complementary, compliant, and accommodating subordinate relationship with hegemonic masculinity. And in the *legitimation* of this relationship of superordination and subordination the meaning and essence of both hegemonic masculinity and emphasized femininity are revealed. This emphasis on hegemony in gender relations underscored the achievement of hegemonic masculinity largely through cultural ascendancy—discursive persuasion—encouraging all to consent to, coalesce around, and embody such unequal gender relations.

Notwithstanding considerable favorable reception of the concept, it nevertheless attracted such criticisms as 1) concerns over the underlying concept of masculinity itself, 2) lack of specificity about who actually represents hegemonic masculinity, 3) whether hegemonic masculinity simply reduces in practice to a reification of power or toxicity, and 4) the concept's unsatisfactory theory of the masculine subject. Having successfully responded to each of these criticisms, Connell and I (2005) reformulated the concept in appropriately significant ways.

First, we discussed what must be retained from the original formulation, clearly noting that the relational idea among hegemonic masculinity, femininity, and nonhegemonic masculinities, as well as the conception that this relationship is a pattern of hegemony—not a pattern of simple domination—have well withstood the test of time. Also well supported historically are the seminal ideas that hegemonic masculinity need not be the commonest and/or the most powerful pattern of masculinity in a particular setting and that any formulation of the concept as simply constituting an assemblage of "masculine" character traits should be thoroughly transcended.

Second, Connell and I nevertheless suggested that a reformulated understanding of hegemonic masculinity must incorporate a more holistic grasp of gender hierarchy that recognizes the agency of subordinated groups as much as the power of hegemonic groups and that appreciates the mutual conditioning (intersectionality) of gender with such other social dynamics as class, race, age, sexuality, and nation. Moreover, we asserted that a more sophisticated treatment of embodiment in hegemonic masculinity was necessary, as well as conceptualizations of how hegemonic masculinity may be challenged, contested, and thus changed.

Finally, Connell and I argued that instead of recognizing simply hegemonic masculinity at only the society-wide level, scholars should analyze empirically existing hegemonic masculinities at three levels: *local* (constructed in arenas of face-to-face interaction of families, organizations, and immediate communities), *re-*

gional (constructed at the society-wide level of culture or nation), and *global* (constructed in such transnational arenas as world politics, business, and media). Obviously, links among these levels exist: global hegemonic masculinities pressure regional and local hegemonic masculinities, and regional hegemonic masculinities provide cultural materials adopted or reworked in global arenas and utilized in local gender dynamics.

With these reformulations in mind, I want to discuss an assortment of selected studies that demonstrate how knowledge on hegemonic masculinity has been constructed differently since 2005. I focus in the next section on two sets of articles (three each) that appropriate the concept of hegemonic masculinity in two distinct and contrasting ways.

CONTRASTING APPROPRIATIONS

The first set demonstrates how hegemonic masculinity is legitimated at the local, regional, and global levels and thus confirms the reformulated model of the concept. The second set appropriates the concept of hegemonic masculinity as exclusively constituting "masculine" character traits and consequently falls back on earlier statements of hegemonic masculinity that solely utilize trait terminology.

Legitimating Hegemonic Masculinity

Since 2005 the vast majority of research examines hegemonic masculinity specifically at the *local* level. An excellent example is the work of Edward Morris (2008; 2012), who studied gender difference in academic perceptions and outcomes at a predominantly white and lower-income rural high school in Kentucky. Appropriating the concept of hegemonic masculinity as a specific contextual pattern of practice that discursively legitimates the subordination of women and femininity to men and masculinity, Morris utilized a mixed methodology by observing in-school interaction, interviewing students (eight boys and seven girls), and analyzing school records and documents. Morris found that girls generally outperformed boys academically and that they had higher ambitions for post-secondary education. Morris demonstrated that in-school interaction positioned masculine qualities as superior to the inferior qualities attached to femininity as well as to certain forms of subordinate masculinity, thereby providing an in-school culturally ascendant discursive justification for unequal gendered social action. The article highlighted how in the localized, face-to-face settings of a rural Kentucky high school, gender inequality was discursively legitimated through the construction of hierarchical socially structured relations between a particular classed, raced, and sexualized hegemonic masculinity and emphasized femininity. Morris concluded that the boys' academic underachievement was embedded in these unequal gender relations.

Research is also examining the construction of *regional* hegemonic masculinities at the level of society-wide culture or nation. An excellent example is a paper by Ronald Weitzer and Charis Kubrin (2009). These authors appropriated the concept of hegemonic masculinity as the discursive subordination of women to men and used the concept to examine all the rap albums that attained platinum status (sales of at least one million copies) from 1992 to 2000. Weitzer and Kubrin chose platinum albums because their numerical success ensured analysis of a rap-music sample that reached a large segment of the U.S. population, thus justifying regional status. Their methodology involved content analysis of a random sample that consisted of 403 songs from 130 different albums. Analysis of the data identified five themes: 1) degradation of women, praise of men; 2) sexual objectification of women, sexual empowerment of men; 3) women as distrustful, men as invulnerable: 4) normality of violence by men, normality of women as victims; and 5) women as prostitutes, men as pimps.

Weitzer and Kubrin's study revealed how much of this rap music discursively constructed a regional form of hegemonic masculinity by depicting men and women as inherently different and unequal and by espousing a set of superior/inferior related gendered qualities for each, for their "appropriate" behavior toward each other, and for the necessity of sanctions if anyone violated the unequal gender relationship. This study demonstrated how within popular culture, through the widespread distribution of rap music, gender inequality was discursively legitimated at the regional level, thereby providing a society-wide cultural rationalization for patriarchal relations. Moreover, Weitzer and Kubrin showed how rap music initially had local roots but came to exercise a society-wide culturally ascendant regional influence on youth of all racial and ethnic groups.

An example of discussions of hegemonic masculinities constructed at the *global* level (in transnational arenas such as world politics, media, and business) is Elizabeth Hatfield's (2010) important piece on the once popular U.S.-based television program *Two and a Half Men*. Hatfield concentrated her scrutiny on the way gender is constructed by the two main characters—Charlie and Alan—who are white, middle-class, professional brothers living together. Hatfield also examined the changing gender constructions by Alan's son, Jake. Since its debut broadcast in 2003, the program led for many years the U.S. sitcom ratings in popularity, being the second most popular (behind *Family Guy*) U.S. television show for males eighteen to twenty-four, averaging approximately 15 million U.S. viewers per week, and it continues to be screened worldwide in at least twenty-four different countries (which approximately triples the number of weekly viewers). Thus, this show continues to have both extensive regional and global influence.

Hatfield employed a content analysis in reviewing 115 sodes of the show, concluding that *Two and a Half Men* off... a media representation of hegemonic masculinity through the gender practices of, and the relationship between, the two main characters. Appropriating hegemonic masculinity as a specific form of masculinity that subordinates both femininity and alternative masculinities, Hatfield found that Charlie constructs hegemonic masculinity and Alan femininity, and in the process Alan's femininity consistently is subordinated to Charlie's hegemonic masculinity.

Hatfield's study admirably demonstrates how a particular sitcom—which has widespread transnational distribution—is an important example of the global legitimation and rationalization of gender inequality through the discursive depiction of a superior/inferior hierarchical relationship between the two main characters. A salient aspect of this sitcom then is how it primarily represents and legitimates an unequal masculine/feminine relationship in and through two assumed male bodies.

"Masculine" Character Traits

Despite the research above, some scholars continue to exclusively equate hegemonic masculinity with certain *"masculine" character traits*. For example, Trevon Logan (2010) studied gay male escorts occupying the dominant position in the male prostitution industry. Logan was interested in how hegemonic masculinity might be reproduced through the practices of these gay male escorts: how these practices might be dominant in the male prostitution business because they allegedly aligned with a society-wide monolithic hegemonic masculinity that subordinated them. Logan (p. 683) appropriated the concept of hegemonic masculinity by identifying such "masculine" traits (that he claimed defined this monolithic hegemonic masculinity) as drive, ambition, self-reliance, aggressiveness, and physical strength, as well as such bodily traits and practices specific to the hegemonically masculine "sexual arena" as physical appearance (muscularity, body size, body hair, and height) and sexual behaviors (sexual dominance, sexual aggressiveness, and penetrative sexual position).

Using a quantitative online data source that described gay male sex workers, Logan found that muscular men enjoyed a dominant position in the male prostitution market (overweight and thin men faced a penalty) that was "consistent with hegemonic masculinity" because "conformity to hegemonic masculine physical norms is well rewarded in the market" (p. 697). Because muscularity signified maleness and dominance, "the premium attached to muscularity in this market is consistent with hegemonic masculinity" (p. 694). Furthermore, according to Logan, the reward of being a "top" (sexually penetrative position) was substantial, as was the penalty for being a "bottom," and thus this finding was "consistent with the theory of hegemonic masculinity" (p. 697). Finally, when Logan studied the interaction of these masculine traits with race, he found that black men were positioned at both extremes: they assigned the largest premiums for top behavior and the largest penalties for bottom behavior. Logan argued that the gay community valued black men who conformed to racial stereotypes of sexual behavior and penalized black men who did not. And Logan (p. 698) concluded that gay men who frequented male escorts "adopt and reiterate hegemonic masculine norms among themselves" and that this in turn was reinforced through the idealized "masculine" traits of dominant-gay-male sex escorts.

A second example of associating hegemonic masculinity with "masculine" traits is an article on aging, independence, and hegemonic masculinity. James Smith and colleagues (2007) specifically examined how men fifty-five years of age and older were encouraged by close acquaintances to seek independence as part of the successful aging process, yet simultaneously were criticized for maintaining their independence from health-service use. These authors appropriated hegemonic masculinity as "the traditional, patriarchal view of men and men's behavior as the most influential and culturally accepted notion of 'manliness,'" that is constituted through "masculine" traits of independence, toughness, assertiveness, emotional restrictiveness, competitiveness, hardiness, aggression, and physical competence (p. 326).

Smith and colleagues interviewed twenty-two men older than fifty-five and twelve men sixty-five or older. For the majority of these men, independence meant self-sufficiency as an indication of their masculinity and the capacity to maintain a good quality of life as they aged. These authors also found that such traits as being tough, strong, and in control were associated with independence and that not wanting to rely on others—and thus avoiding help seeking and health-service use—was a consistent theme influencing the men's ability to enact "masculine" traits.

In addition to masculinity, the ability to function independently also was a reflection of one's quality of life. Smith and colleagues found that maintaining daily physical and cognitive functioning was important for supporting the men's independent state of being but also reflected the way they positioned themselves as men. These authors concluded that the concern of men fifty-five and older about independence reflected both their identity as men and their identity as older people. For these subjects, independence was a characteristic of masculine identity and a marker of successful aging, both of which were important to the assessment of how they negotiated help seeking and health-service use.

Finally, a third example is an article written by Elizabeth Gage (2008) who examined the impact that male college athletes' participation in different sports had on their gender attitudes, hegemonic masculinity, sexual behavior, and sexual aggression. Gage (p. 1018) argued that her study offered "an opportunity to refine understanding of what it is about sports participation that leads to hegemonic masculinity and sexual aggression." Unfortunately, this study never formally defined hegemonic masculinity yet created the impression that the concept amounted to specific toxic character traits.

By means of a survey, Gage measured the "gender role identification," "attitudes toward women," "hypermasculinity," and "sexual behavior, sexual aggression, and sexual orientation" of 148 college males, both athletes (football, tennis, and track and field) and nonathletes. Gage found that football players scored significantly higher on hypermasculinity and sexual aggression scales (toxic traits) than did the athletes in the other two sports but scored significantly lower than the same athletes on attitudes-toward-women scales (harmless traits). A similar pattern emerged when football players were compared to nonathletes, but fewer significant differences were noted between nonathletes and tennis and track and field athletes.

Despite never actually defining or measuring hegemonic masculinity, Gage (p. 1029) concluded that her research on the role that participation in sports—especially football—had on college males indicated a "more nuanced understanding of the relationship between hegemonic masculinity, attitudes toward women, and violence against women." But the most we can reasonably deduce from this article is that for Gage, hegemonic masculinity was reduced to such toxic, hypermasculine character traits as "negative attitudes toward women," "violence as manly," and "calloused sex attitudes toward women" that primarily were embodied in football players.

Summary

No social science concept is ever fixed and no social science scholar has a monopoly on its correct use. Nevertheless, the concept of hegemonic masculinity was originally formulated to conceptualize how patriarchal relations are *legitimated* throughout society. The juxtaposition presented here of two contrasting appropriations of the concept demonstrates how the meaning of hegemonic masculinity has differed within recently published articles. The first three articles confirm the Connell and Messerschmidt (2005) reformulation of the concept by demonstrating that empirically existing hegemonic masculinities exist at local, regional, and global levels; that hegemonic masculinities are formed through an unequal and hierarchical relationship between masculinities and femininities (even though femininities may be constructed in and through male bodies); and that through this relationship hegemonic masculinities discursively circulate a culturally ascendant legitimating justification for gender inequality. The second three articles reveal that the meaning of the concept continues to be a troubled area in research on hegemonic masculinity. Although these latter three articles are similar in their concentration on "masculine" traits, they differ in the way they associate these traits with hegemonic masculinity: as constituting *widespread* character traits, as equated with the most *influential* manliness, and as consisting of exclusively specific *toxic* traits consolidated in a particular group of men (football players).

NEW DIRECTIONS

Recent research on hegemonic masculinity additionally takes the engendering of gendered knowledge in promising new directions. This new directions work demonstrates 1) how women contribute to the *cultivation* of hegemonic masculinity, 2) how hegemonic masculinity actually can be *contested* and thus challenged, and 3) how neoliberal globalization influences the orchestration of hegemonic and nonhegemonic masculinities in *periphery* countries. Here I focus on six articles (three sets of two) that represent these trends.

Cultivation

Research is emerging that features how the agency of women contributes to the *cultivation* of hegemonic masculinity. For example, Kirsten Talbot and Michael Quayle (2010) argued that the production of hegemonic masculinities requires "at least some kind of 'buy-in' from women" and that thus under certain circumstances and in specific situations women construct "emphasized femininities" whereby they "contribute to the perpetuation of oppressive gender relations and identities" (p. 256). Through in-depth interviews and an extensive focus group session with five heterosexual, middle-class, and university undergraduate South African women, Talbot and Quayle explored interviewee involvement in a variety of localized contexts—work, social, romantic, and family—and found that the five women uniformly grouped these four contexts into two parts: "work and social" versus "romantic and family" situations. In each part the women reported supporting specific and unique types of gender relations; that is, they identified certain inviolable masculine and feminine qualities that each considered essential to each situation.

In romantic and family situations, the women argued that men should be in control and dominant, should financially provide for family members, and should protect those in their care. In work and social settings, however, the women desired their male workmates and male friends to possess masculine characteristics centering on platonic, friendly, equal relationships. In work and social relationships with men, male passivity was valued and male agency was undesirable; in romantic and family relationships, agency was valued and passivity was undesirable. In work and social contexts, then, the women expected to be treated in an egalitarian and gender-progressive manner, they considered romantic and family masculine features as "violations," and they valued those masculine features that "violated" hegemonic masculine qualities.

Although not a representative sample, the interviewees in this study supported and expected different types of gender relations in different local contexts. Accordingly, this study demonstrated how various forms of gender relations might be produced contextually and validated by both men *and* women and how women might construct differing forms of femininities—emphasized and liberated—in differing contexts as they recognize and support situational masculinities. And in regard to the specific cultivation of hegemonic masculinity, the women in this study were "particularly willing to accept subjugation to engage in ideals of romantic partnership congruent with emphasized femininity" and thereby legitimate gender hegemony (p. 255).

As a second example, in an article on hegemonic masculinity and the profession of veterinary medicine Leslie Irvine and Jenny Vermilya (2010) demonstrate that, despite contemporary veterinary medicine being numerically dominated by women, it is the women in this profession who often sustain, justify, and preserve hegemonic masculinity. Through interviews with twenty-two women who were practicing veterinarians or veterinary students, Irvine and Vermilya found that certain "inferior" gendered characteristics, such as nurturance, compassion, and emotionality traditionally were attached to female veterinarians. The women veterinarians interviewed actually placed little value on these particular characteristics and, in fact, they distanced themselves from these traits through their on-the-job practices. The women veterinarians instead constructed practices traditionally viewed by the profession as "superior," such as emphasizing science rather than nurturance, insensitivity in place of compassion, and control instead of emotionality. Irvine and Vermilya demonstrated how women veterinarians participated in "the patterns of practice that sustain and justify the status quo, and thus preserve hegemonic masculinity" (p. 74). These women appropriated the same practices that men had long used to keep women out of the profession and therefore exemplified how hegemonic masculinity might be cultivated by those deemed subordinate and with interests at odds with that hegemonic masculinity. The consequences of hegemonic masculinity in this profession actually lower salaries for women relative to men, underrepresent women in the administration of veterinary schools, concentrate women in companion-animal services, and maintain low numbers of women who own veterinary practices.

Contestation

Always open to challenge when contested, hegemonic masculinities often inspire new strategies in gender relations and result in new configurations of hegemonic masculinities. For example, in an examination of autobiographical accounts of British soldiers involved in peacekeeping duties in Bosnia in the 1990s, Claire Duncanson (2009) explored whether or not a subsequent peace-keeping masculinity challenged the local hegemonic masculinity of the British military. Duncanson identified the British military hegemonic masculinity as consisting of the brave, strong, and tough masculine soldier/protector in contrast to the timid, weak, and tender feminine wife/mother in need of protection.

Through an analysis of four autobiographical accounts of British soldiers/officers involved in peacekeeping missions (formal and informal activities designed to prevent, halt, or resolve conflicts) in Bosnia, Duncanson found first that each of these soldiers experienced both *emasculating* and *masculinizing* aspects of peacekeeping: regarding the former, each soldier considered peacekeeping inferior, frustrating, and less masculine than "real fighting"; concerning the latter, each attempted therefore to position peacekeeping as one-hundred-percent masculine behavior. For Duncanson, the former (emasculation) reinforced the local military hegemonic masculinity but the latter (masculinist) both disrupted that hegemonic masculinity and attempted to position peacemaking masculinity as a new form of localized hegemonic masculinity in the British military. As Duncanson (p. 69) explained, "When soldiers valorize peacekeeping tasks as masculine, they are not only asserting that there is another way to be a 'real man'; they are asserting that it is *the* way." Although all the soldiers/officers regarded peacekeeping as often emasculating, they simultaneously constructed peacekeeping as masculine by claiming that actually it was tougher, more dangerous, and more challenging than participating in war.

At the same time, these soldiers/officers did not challenge the notion of women solely as wives and mothers in need of protection, and they feminized Balkan male soldiers as weak, irrational, and emotional while masculinizing themselves as controlled, civilized, and intelligent. Peacekeeping masculinity then challenged traditional British localized military hegemonic masculinity yet simultaneously was constructed in relation to subordinate racialized and feminized "Others." The end result was a new form of hegemonic masculinity that discursively legitimated hierarchical gender relations between men and women, between masculinity and femininity, and among masculinities.

A second example of the contestation of hegemonic masculinity is a study of high school rugby in Australia by Richard Light (2007), who appropriated hegemonic masculinity as a localized discourse in the particular setting of the high school and operated "at an unquestioned, common-sense level" (p. 323). Light argued that this particular hegemonic masculine discourse shaped the performance of the high school rugby team members by emphasizing physical force and power during play instead of skills and tactical knowledge. Through interviews with team members and the coach, as well as observations of practices and games, Light found that the majority of players described this discursive approach to the sport as "no mistakes" rugby, which was "highly structured, predictable, and heavy" (p. 329). The hegemonic masculine discourse encouraged players to take an instrumental view of their bodies as weapons to dominate and actually injure opponents. Value was placed on employing powerful and purposeful physical contact, bodily force, and mastery to overcome the opposition; to take control of "enemy" territory on the field; and to move the team forward throughout the season. Players were thus compelled to embody "heavy contact" so as to establish a superior power position over opponents—there was little room allowed for player autonomy, independence, and creativity in generating and utilizing space.

Within the confines of the high school setting, then, a powerful discourse emphasized a characteristic hard and tough hegemonic masculinity that the boys on the rugby team felt obliged to reproduce. No boy wanted to "let down the tradition" of the school, and this credo made it difficult for any player to challenge the contextual hegemonically masculine discourse in any explicit way. And because of its power, the boys reproduced this particular pattern of hegemonic masculinity over generations.

Nevertheless, and despite the struggle, the boys did attempt to contest the no mistakes form of rugby through a much-less-structured and more creative style of play. During a two-week break at school the team participated in a rugby tournament, and it was here that the players decided collectively to change their style of play in a way that allowed more risk-taking on the field and more support for each other when mistakes occurred. The new style also involved much less structure, better communication, respectful understanding among players, and increased excitement—enthusiasm for the new "open" rugby as opposed to the "no mistakes" rugby was dramatic. And because of the success with the new style of play, following the tournament the coach decided to allow the team to play open rugby in the remaining games of the season. Yet owing to an important loss to a regular season team, school administrators and coaches quickly dropped the new style of play. Again, Light attributed this to how deeply embedded the hegemonic masculine discourse was in the culture of the school. In other words, although the players attempted to mount a new form of masculinity that contested the established no mistakes rugby, the traditional hegemonic masculine discourse was far too entrenched in the school culture for any new hegemonic masculinity to emerge. Accordingly, Light insightfully documented the social processes involved in a localized struggle over hegemony and the reinstallment of a traditional hegemonic masculinity that had been contested and briefly displaced.

Periphery

Research also is appearing that highlights how neoliberal globalization influences the construction of hegemonic and nonhegemonic masculinities in *periphery* countries, such as those in Asia, Africa, and Central and Latin America. An excellent example is a study that utilized a mixed methodology—a survey, focus group discussions, and interviews. In this article, Christian Groes-Green (2009) examined the impact of neoliberal globalization on both urban middle-class and urban working-class young men (ages sixteen to twenty-three) in Maputo, Mozambique. Groes-Green found that in the local arena of Maputo, an established form of hegemonic masculinity involved men providing economically for their female partners and families, a practice that primarily defined hierarchical relations between them. Although both the middle-class and working-class young men Groes-Green studied intended to construct such hierarchical gender relations, with the arrival of neoliberal globalization only the former were able to live up to this particular hegemonic masculinity.

In 1987 the Mozambican government, through economic support from the World Bank and the International Monetary Fund, allowed considerable foreign business investment into the country. This policy subsequently heralded a growing middle class with access to higher education, steady and secure jobs, and excellent incomes. Nevertheless, the downside of this development was economic impoverishment of the majority of the population, mass unemployment among primarily working-class youth, and an increasing gap between the middle and working classes.

During his fieldwork, Groes-Green observed how middle-class and working-class young men constructed different hegemonic masculinities, and he attributed these contrasting masculinities to the neoliberal economic changes impacting Maputo. In particular, the middle-class young men had easy access to higher education, stable employment, and high incomes. Consequently, they were able to easily attract young women as partners who also supported hierarchical gender relations—these young men effortlessly constructed this particular type of localized hegemonic masculinity.

In contrast the working-class young men, who experienced much less access to higher education as well as escalating unemployment rates, were unable to live up to the standards of hegemonic masculinity in this localized environment. And as Groes-Green (p. 299) put it, these men developed "a masculinity that takes the body and its physical powers as its sources." In the absence of higher education, stable jobs, and an adequate income, these working-class men engaged in two specific "corporeal performances" to construct masculine power relations over their female partners. The first corporeal performance involved their becoming preoccupied with particular "sexual techniques" (such as consuming large quantities of aphrodisiacs), allegedly to increase their sexual skills and sexual stamina and thereby provide "a gateway to staying in power" by preserving a sense of superiority over their partner by managing her sexual satisfaction (p. 298). The second corporeal performance involved some of these men increasingly engaging in physical violence against their female partner primarily to "make her respect you" (p. 294). These two identified corporeal performances were impetuous attempts to somehow legitimate patriarchal relations through particular practices of sexuality and violence at the local level.

For Groes-Green, then, the two masculine corporeal performances were bifurcated reactions to the inability of these young men to construct and legitimate traditional hegemonic masculinity because of neoliberal-produced poverty-stricken circumstances. Both forms of corporeal performances became an "option to which poor young men in Maputo resort when their hegemony (i.e., their 'taken for granted' authority based on stable jobs and financial abilities) is contested" (p. 296).

Similarly, Chad Broughton (2008) examined how neoliberal globalization in Mexico created a novel northward mass departure from the Mexican southern states by working-age men and women. In particular, Broughton analyzed how economically dislocated southern Mexican men negotiated hegemonic masculinity while confronting extraordinary pressure to migrate as well as the gendered strategies, practices, and identities they adopted during the undertaking.

Following implementation of the North American Free Trade Agreement (NAFTA) on January 1, 1994, numerous trade barriers to foreign investment in Mexico were removed; NAFTA created the conditions for the concentration and acceleration of foreign investment and manufacturing growth at the U.S.-Mexico border, thereby "creating a strong draw for job-hungry, impoverished Mexicans" (p. 570). Moreover, NAFTA opened Mexico's agricultural sector to U.S. agribusiness by increasing trade quotas and decreasing tariffs for major crops (such as corn), necessarily compressing rural economies and boosting northern migration.

Through life-history interviews of sixteen low-income men (eighteen to forty-two years old) who contemplated migrating north from southern Mexico, Broughton found that these men constructed three differing masculinities in reaction to migration pressures in neoliberal Mexico. Drawing on a specific localized hegemonic masculinity that emphasized hierarchical gender relations in the family and vigilant fathering, these men deployed what Broughton labeled "traditionalist," "adventurer," and "breadwinner" masculinities, all of which provided differing gendered responses "to realizing both instrumental and identity goals in a time of rapid and wrenching change" (p. 585).

The *traditionalist* emphasized maintaining the established local hegemonic masculinity primarily through family cohesion. Viewing the border as a "minefield of moral hazards," the traditionalist decided to endure destitution in the south and refrain from migrating in order to protect his family from such dangers up north. The traditionalist then maintained local hegemonic masculinity in his southern home "in spite of political and economic forces working against the maintenance of such ideals" (p. 577).

For the *adventurer*, the northern border and beyond offered a place to earn considerable money and to "prove" his masculinity in new ways, such as through seeking thrills and breaking free from the inflexibility of rural life. Rejecting the localized notion of hegemonic masculinity, migration to the north presented a progressive, avant-garde means to survive economic disorder by upgrading one's masculine status and assessing his bravery. It proffered a "new and exciting life away from the limitations of a neglected and declining rural Mexico" (p. 585).

Finally, like the adventurer, the *breadwinner* migrated to the north, yet unlike the adventurer such migration was a reluctant but necessary choice under desperate circumstances—he had to do so to adequately provide for his wife and children. The breadwinner coped with "symbolic indignities" so that he could acquire sufficient economic resources that would conceivably promote social mobility for his entire family. The breadwinner accepted work at or beyond the border "as an inescapable duty" so that his family would enjoy a higher standard of living (p. 585).

Broughton's study then demonstrated how low-income Mexican men experiencing economic dislocation intrinsic to neoliberal Mexico negotiated with a specific localized hegemonic masculinity discursively and in the process orchestrated old and new hegemonic and new nonhegemonic masculine configurations. This differing process of masculine identity formation involved much more than simply instrumental calculations; these men had to "make sense of the migration experience as men and arrive at specific and adaptive gendered strategies and decisions regarding northward migration" (p. 586). One of the important aspects of this article was its demonstration of how specific forms of complicity (traditionalist and breadwinner) with, and resistance (adventurer) to, a localized hegemonic masculinity discourse were constructed under identical neoliberal conditions.

Summary

These six studies have engendered gender knowledge in new and innovative ways by 1) recognizing how under certain situations women might be a salient factor in the cultivation of hegemonic masculinities, 2) revealing how hegemonic masculinities may be open to challenge and possibly reproduced in new form, and 3) demonstrating how neoliberal globalization impacts the construction of various forms of hegemonic and nonhegemonic masculinities in periphery countries. All six articles illustrate contemporary creative scholarship that contributes distinctively to academic gendered knowledge on hegemonic masculinity. The two articles on cultivation show that in studies of hegemonic masculinities, the focus can no longer center exclusively on men and instead must give much closer attention to both the practices of women and the social interplay of femininities and masculinities. Several of the new directions pieces document various ways hegemonic masculinities have been contested, resulting in the construction of new strategies of patriarchal relations and thus redefinitions of hegemonic masculinities. And within periphery countries experiencing the effects of neoliberal globalization, the articles reveal how attempts by men at the individual level to maintain localized power relations over women might occur and further display how certain alternative nonhegemonic masculinities might arise under such conditions. Each article in its own particular way then breaks new ground by concentrating on academic domains that previously have been disregarded (cultivation and contestation) or seemingly deemed incapable of exploration and analysis (periphery). This work can inspire additional gender research that further extends our knowledge in similar and/or previously unexplored areas.

In sum, then, the primary purpose of this first chapter is to set the stage for the remaining chapters by assessing the academic *appropriation* of the reformulated concept of hegemonic masculinity and the processes involved in gendered knowledge construction. The analysis reveals first that contrasting interpretations of the concept by gender scholars persist and that such disparities have crept into the accepted academic accumulation of gendered knowledge. Published articles hold an extremely salient position in academic gendered knowledge construction, and the publication of an article in an accepted academic journal sanctions its scholarly stature. It is through such journals that specific forms of gendered knowledge are substantiated academically and upon such journal articles that the academic community depends for the dissemination of new forms of gendered knowledge.

Nevertheless, a published journal article results from more than the author's research and writing. As with all forms of social action, the publishing of an academic journal article involves interaction among editor(s), reviewers, and the author(s), and such interaction indispensably shapes the ultimate content of the final published draft. Published academic articles, then, are shaped so that they conform to the parameters fixed by the particular reviewers and editors. Contrasting and disparate forms of gendered knowledge—here regarding conceptualizations of hegemonic masculinity—thereby result from interaction among a variety of editors, reviewers, and authors.

More than seventeen years ago, Martin (1998) raised the issue of inconsistent appropriations of the concept of hegemonic masculinity, insightfully observing that some scholars equated the concept with a fixed type of masculinity or with whatever type of masculinity that happened to be dominant at a particular time and place. More recently, Beasley (2008; 2013; Elias and Beasley, 2009) labeled such inconsistent appropriations "slippage," arguing that "dominant" forms of masculinity—such as those that are the most culturally celebrated or the most common in particular settings—may actually do little to legitimate men's power over women and that some masculinities that legitimate men's power actually may be culturally marginalized. Similarly, Schippers (2007) argued that it is essential to distinguish masculinities that legitimate men's power from those that do not.

Although these scholars have correctly pointed to the relevant ambiguities in appropriations of the concept, what this chapter illustrates is that sundry scholars are demonstrating impressively through their published academic articles how specific hierarchical gender relationships between men and women, between masculinity and femininity, and among masculinities are legitimated—in my view superbly capturing certain of the essential features of the omnipresent reproduction of patriarchal relations. Additionally, these articles reveal in various ways how hegemonic masculinities express models of gender relations that articulate with the practical constitution of masculine and feminine ways of living in everyday circumstances. To the extent they do this, they contribute to our understanding of the legitimation and stabilization of patriarchal relations locally, regionally, and globally.

Notwithstanding, "slippage" in the conception of hegemonic masculinity in this chapter has centered exclusively on equating the concept with "masculine" character traits. However, this particular form of slippage is not solely a matter of individual interpretation of the concept. Within the articles examined, there remains a fundamental *collective* intellectual tendency by numerous editors, reviewers, and authors "to read 'hegemonic masculinity' as a static character type, that is, to psychologize the idea and ignore the whole question of gender dynamics" (Connell, 2008: 245). The articles in this study that conceptualize hegemonic masculinity in this way—typified by Logan, Smith and colleagues, and Gage—unquestionably offer intriguing insight into the adoption of certain "masculine" traits by particular groups of men. Nevertheless, in terms of *hegemony* in patriarchal relations that is explicit in the concept of hegemonic masculinity, their presentation is noticeably abbreviated. That is, their work calls for an additional step to be taken, involving an analysis of the downstream consequences of how the particular "masculine" traits actually legitimate gender inequality and the subordination of women, femininities, and nonhegemonic masculinities. And the articles by Morris, Weitzer and Kubrin, Hatfield, Talbot and Quayle, Duncanson, and others discussed herein represent some promising approaches as to how such downstreaming can be accomplished. Unfortunately, it is impossible to do this vital extended analysis on Gage's data because examination of the legitimation of patriarchal relations cannot methodologically be well articulated and formulated.

Accordingly, I agree with Schippers (2007) that to elucidate the significance and salience of hegemonic masculinities, gender scholars—which includes editors, reviewers, and authors—must

distinguish masculinities that legitimate a hierarchical relationship between men and women, between masculinity and femininity, and among masculinities from those that do not. Hegemonic
masculinities are unique among the diversity of masculinities, and
making this distinction unambiguous will enable scholars to recognize and research various forms of mundane, run-of-the-mill,
nonhegemonic masculinities that are constructed outside hegemonic relations, such as those constructed by the older men in
the Smith and colleagues article, as well as risky and daring types
of masculinities, such as the adventurer masculinity discussed by
Broughton. Labeling these particular types of masculinities "hegemonic masculinity" confounds any analysis as to how nonhegemonic masculinities differ from hegemonic masculinities, thereby
essentially confusing and obscuring the academic engendering of
gendered knowledge.

Moreover, certain masculinities (without legitimating patriarchal relations) may be dominant and/or dominating. In this regard, I (Messerschmidt, 2010; 2012; 2014) recently distinguished—and throughout this book I will elaborate on—these
two types of nonhegemonic masculinities: "dominant" masculinities refer to the most powerful or the most widespread types in
the sense of being the most celebrated, common, or current
forms of masculinity in a specific social setting; "dominating" masculinities involve commanding and controlling specific interactions and exercising power and control over people and events—
"calling the shots" and "running the show." Neither dominant nor
dominating masculinities necessarily legitimate hierarchical gender relations between men and women, between masculinity and
femininity, and among masculinities. Even though at times hegemonic masculinities also may be dominant and/or dominating,
these latter masculinities are never hegemonic if they fail culturally to legitimate patriarchal relations (see further Beasley, 2008;
2013). To conceptualize fully hegemonic masculinities, then,

scholars must unravel dominant, dominating, and other types of nonhegemonic masculinities from hegemonic masculinities. I define "hegemonic masculinity" as those masculinities that *legitimate* an unequal *relationship* between men and women, masculinity and femininity, and among masculinities. The emphasis on *hegemony* underscores the achievement of hegemonic masculinity through cultural influence and thus discursive persuasion, encouraging consent and compliance—rather than direct control and commands—to unequal gender relations. And this distinction between hegemonic and nonhegemonic masculinities further facilitates the discovery and identification of "positive masculinities," or those that actually may help to legitimate an egalitarian relationship between men and women, between masculinity and femininity, and among masculinities. (For examples of positive masculinities, see the work of Deutsch (1999), Lorber (2005), and Schippers (2007) as well as chapter 3.)

Finally, although identifying a *single* society-wide or global "ascendant" hegemonic masculinity may be possible, no one to date has successfully done so. This is probably the case because it is extremely difficult to measure such ascendancy and thereby determine which particular masculinity—among the whole variety in the offering—is indeed *the* ascendant hegemonic masculinity. Until a method is devised for determining exactly which masculinity is *the* hegemonic ascendant, we must speak of hegemonic masculinity—as the reformulated concept suggests and the current evidence documents—wholly in plural terms, analyzing hegemonic masculin*ies* at the local, regional, and global levels. Such research will provide a growing expansion of our understanding of the pervasive and omnipresent nature of how hegemonic masculinity and thus patriarchal relations are legitimized and solidified from the local to the global. And in the chapters that follow I contribute to the above research on hegemonic and nonhegemonic masculinities by taking the engendering of gender knowledge in new directions.

2

MASCULINITIES AS STRUCTURED ACTION

To grasp the notion of "masculinities as structured action" we must turn to structured action theory that has been employed previously (Messerschmidt, 1993; 1997; 2000; 2004; 2010; 2012; 2014) in understanding the relationship among sex, gender, race, class, and sexuality. In this book I exclusively concentrate on sex, gender, and sexuality and I begin chapter 2 by explaining how structured action theory conceptualizes "doing" sex, gender, and sexuality.

DOING SEX, GENDER, AND SEXUALITY

Reflecting various theoretical origins (Archer, 2003; 2007; 2012; Connell, 1987; 1995; Giddens, 1976; 1984; Goffman, 1963; 1972; 1979; Kessler and McKenna, 1978; Mouzelis, 2008; Sartre, 1956; West and Fenstermaker, 1995; West and Zimmerman, 1987), structured action theory emphasizes the construction of sex, gender, and sexuality as situated social, interactional, and embodied accomplishments. In other words, sex, gender, and sexuality grow out of embodied social practices in specific social structural settings and serve to inform such practices in reciprocal relation.

Regarding *sex*, historical and social conditions shape the character and definition of sex (social identification as "male" or "female"). Sex and its meanings are given concrete expression by the specific social relations and historical context in which they are embedded. Historical studies on the definition of sex show its clear association with sexuality, and gender has proved always to be already involved. The work of Thomas Laqueur (1990) is exemplary in this regard, and in his important book, *Making Sex*, he shows that for two thousand years a "one-sex model" dominated scientific and popular thought in which male and female bodies were not conceptualized in terms of difference. From antiquity to the beginning of the seventeenth century, male and female bodies were seen as having the same body parts, even in terms of genitalia, with the vagina regarded as an interior penis, the vulva as foreskin, the uterus as scrotum, and the ovaries as testicles. Women thus had the same body as men but the positioning of its parts was different: as one doggerel verse of the period stated, "women are but men turned outside in" (p. 4). In the "one-sex model" the sexes were not seen as different in *kind* but rather in *degree*—woman simply was a lesser form of man. And as Laqueur (p. 8) explains, "*Sex*, or the body, must be understood as the epiphenomenon, while *gender*, what we would take to be a cultural category, was primary or 'real.'" Inequality was imposed on bodies from the outside and seen as God's "marker" of a male and female distinction. To be a man or a woman was to have a specific place in society decreed by God, "not to *be* organically one or the other of two incommensurable sexes. Sex before the seventeenth century, in other words, was still a sociological and not an ontological category" (p. 8).

What emerged after the Enlightenment was a "two-sex model" involving a foundational dichotomy between now two and only two distinct and opposite sexes, as no longer did scientific and popular thought "regard woman as a lesser version of man along a vertical axis of infinite gradations but rather an altogether different creature along a horizontal axis whose middle ground was largely empty" (p. 148). And Michel Foucault's (1980: vii) well-known discussion of the "hermaphrodite" *Herculine Barbin* (what is referred today as the intersexed), demonstrates that by the mid-1800s there was no allowance for any human being to occupy a "middle ground" through "a mixture of two sexes in a single body," which consequently limited "the free choice of indeterminate individuals" and thus henceforth "everybody was to have one and only one sex." Individuals accepted previously as representatives of the "middle ground" ("hermaphrodites") were now required to submit to expert medical diagnosis to uncover their "true" sex. As Foucault (p. vii) continues:

> Everybody was to have his or her primary, profound, determined and determining sexual identity; as for the elements of the other sex that might appear, they could only be accidental, superficial, or even quite simply illusory. From the medical point of view, this meant that when confronted with a hermaphrodite, the doctor was no longer concerned with recognizing the presence of the two sexes, juxtaposed or intermingled, or with knowing which of the two prevailed over the other, but rather with deciphering the true sex that was hidden beneath ambiguous appearances.

Arguably, then, under the "two-sex model" it became commonplace to view *the* male sex and *the* female sex as "different in every conceivable aspects of body and soul, in every physical and moral aspect—an anatomy and physiology of incommensurability replaced a metaphysics of hierarchy in the representation of woman in relation to man" (Laqueur, 1990: 5–6).

Predictably, these two now fixed, incommensurable, opposite sexes also are conceptualized as *the* source of the political, economic, and cultural lives of men and women (gender and sexuality), since "biology—the stable, ahistorical, sexed body—is understood to be the epistemic foundation for prescriptive claims about the social order" (p. 6). To be sure, it was now understood as "natural" that women are, for example, passive, submissive, and vulnerable and men are, for example, active, aggressive, and perilous. And given that anatomy is now destiny, a heterosexual instinct to procreate proceeds from the body and is "the natural state of the architecture of two incommensurable opposite sexes" (p. 233).

The shift in thinking to a "two-sex model," consisting now of two different types of humans with complementary heterosexual natures and desires, corresponded to the emergence of the public/private split: It was now "natural" for men to enter the public realm of society and it was "natural" for women to remain in the private sphere. Explaining these distinct gendered spaces was "resolved by grounding social and cultural differentiation of the sexes in a biology of incommensurability" (Laqueur, 1990: 19). In other words, "gender" and "sexuality" became subordinated to "sex" and biology was now primary: *the* foundation of difference and inequality between men and women.

Laqueur makes clear that the change to a two-sex model was not the result of advances in science, inasmuch as the reevaluation of the body as primary occurred approximately one hundred years before alleged supporting scientific discoveries appeared. And although anatomical and physiological differences clearly exist between male and female bodies, what counts as "sex" is determined socially. In short, natural scientists had no interest in "seeing" two distinct sexes at the anatomical and concrete physiological level "until such differences became politically important" and "sex" therefore became "explicable only within the context of battles over gender and power" (pp. 10, 11).

The historical work of both Laqueur and Foucault suggests that "sex differences" do not naturally precede "gender and sexual differences." And as Wendy Cealey Harrison (2006) insightfully observes, it is virtually impossible to ever entirely separate the body and our understanding of it from its socially determined milieu. Arguably, what is now necessary is a reconceptualization of "the taken-for-grantedness of 'sex' as a form of categorization for human beings and examining the ways in which such a categorization is built" (p. 43).

Following this suggestion by Cealey Harrison, it is important to recognize that in an important early work Suzanne Kessler and Wendy McKenna (1978) argued that social action is constructed through taken-for-granted discourses, or what they call "incorrigible propositions." Our belief in two objectively real, biologically created constant yet opposite sexes is a telling discourse. We assume there are only two sexes; each person is simply an example of one or the other. In other words, we construct a sex dichotomy in which no dichotomy holds biologically, historically, cross-culturally, and contemporaneously (Messerschmidt, 2004).

The key process in the social construction of the sex dichotomy is the active way we decide what sex a person is (Kessler and McKenna, 1978: 1–20). A significant part of this sex attribution process is the notion that men have penises and women do not. We consider genitals the ultimate criterion in making sex assignments; yet, in our daily interactions we continually make sex attributions with a complete lack of information about others' genitals. Our recognition of another's sex is dependent upon the exhibit of such bodily characteristics as speech, hair, clothing, physical appearance, and other aspects of personal front—through this embodied presentation we "do" sex and it is this doing that becomes a substitute for the concealed genitalia.

Nevertheless, *doing gender* (West and Zimmerman, 1987) entails considerably more than the "social emblems" representing membership in one of two sex categories. Rather, the social construction of gender involves a situated social, interactional, and embodied accomplishment. Gender grows out of social practices

in specific settings and serves to inform such practices in reciprocal relation. Although "sex" defines social identification as "male"
or "female," "doing gender" systematically corroborates and qual-
ifies that sex identification and category through embodied social
interaction. We "do" gender as a demonstration of our self-attribution as "male" or "female" and in turn that "doing" validates our
"sex" identity. In effect, there is a plurality of forms in which
gender is constructed: we coordinate our activities to "do" gender
in situational ways (West and Zimmerman, 1987).

Accordingly, early gender development in childhood occurs
through an interactive process between child and parents, other
children, and other adults. By reason of this interaction with others—and the social structures this interaction constitutes—children (for the most part) undertake to practice what is being
preached, represented, and structured. Raewyn Connell defines
the proactive adoption of specific embodied gender practices as
the "moment of engagement," the moment when an individual
initiates a project of masculinity or femininity as his or her own
(1995: 122). The young child has in effect located him- or herself
in relation to others within a sexed and gendered structured field
(Jackson, 2007). Children negotiate the socially structured sexed
and gendered practices and their accompanying discourses that
are prevalent and attributed as such in their particular milieu(s)
and, in so doing, commit themselves to a *fundamental project* of
sex and gender self-attribution—for example, "I'm a boy" or "I'm
a girl." This fundamental self-attribution as a boy or as a girl is the
primary mode by which agents choose to relate to the world and
to express themselves in it, and thus serves as an important constraint and enabler in the social construction of sex, gender, and
sexuality. What makes us human is the fact that we construct
ourselves by making reflexive choices that transcend given
circumstances and propel us into a future that is defined by the
consequences of those choices. Doing sex and gender—normally

concurrently—is a continuing process in which agents construct patterns of embodied presentations and practices that suggest a particular sex and gender in specific settings and, consequently, project themselves into a future where new situations are encountered and subsequently new reflexive choices are made (Connell, 1995). There exists a certain degree of unity and coherence to one's fundamental sex and gender project in the sense that we tend to embody this particular sexed and gendered self—for example, "I'm a boy" or "I'm a girl"—over time and space.

Nevertheless, and although agents construct a fundamental project as either male or female, the actual accomplishment of gender may vary situationally—that is, gender is renegotiated continuously through social interaction and, therefore, one's gendered self may be fraught with contradictions and diversity in gender strategies and practices. For example, agents may situationally construct a specific fundamental gender project (for example, masculine) that contradicts their bodily sex category (for example, female).

Sexuality involves all erotic and nonerotic aspects of social life and social being that relate to bodily attraction or intimate bodily contact between individuals, such as arousal, desire, practice, discourse, interaction, relationship, and identity (see Jackson and Scott, 2010). "Doing" sexuality encompasses the same interactional processes discussed above for doing gender and therefore likewise involves children initially acquiring knowledge primarily about heterosexuality through structured interaction with mothers, fathers, other children, and other adults. This initial process involves the acquisition of mostly nonerotic forms of heterosexual discursive knowledge, such as male-female marital relationships that suggest this is "where babies come from." However, to adopt such rudimentary heterosexual discursive knowledge, "doing sex" must take primacy. As Stevi Jackson and Sue Scott (2010: 91–92) point out, "We recognize someone as male or female before we make assumptions about heterosexuality or homosexuality; we cannot logically do otherwise." The homosexual/heterosexual socially structured dichotomy hinges on meaningful sexed categories, "on being able to 'see' two men or two women as 'the same' and a man and a woman as 'different'" (p. 92). The notion of two and only two sex categories then establishes the discursive rationale for the homosexual/heterosexual socially structured dichotomy.

Once children begin to develop a sense of the erotic aspects of sexuality—which usually occurs through interaction with peers in secondary school—their sense-making is governed by their embodied sexed and gendered self (Jackson, 2007). "Doing" sex, gender, and sexuality intersect here, so that our conceptualization of sex and gender impacts our understanding and practice of sexuality (both the erotic and the nonerotic aspects) and it is through sexual practices (once again both the erotic and the nonerotic) that we validate sex and gender. Agents adopt embodied sexual practices as a "moment of engagement," a moment when the individual begins to affix a specific sexual project to their fundamental sex and gender project, constructing, for example, heteromasculine and heterofeminine identities. Sex, gender, and sexuality are produced and reproduced by embodied individuals, and interaction with others is essential to one's ability to negotiate and fit in to ongoing and situationally structured patterns of sex, gender, and sexuality.

Crucial to this negotiation and "fitting in" is the notion of "accountability" (West and Zimmerman, 1987; Hollander, 2013). Accountability—as the cornerstone of social structural reproduction—refers to individuals anticipating assessment of their behavior and therefore they configure and orchestrate their embodied actions in relation to how such actions may be interpreted by others in the particular social context in which they occur. In other words, in their daily activities agents attempt to be identified bodily as "female" or "male" through sex, gender, and sexual practices. Within socially structured interaction, then, we encourage and expect others to attribute to us a particular sex category— to avoid negative assessments—and we facilitate the ongoing task of accountability through demonstrating that we are male or female by means of concocted practices that may be interpreted accordingly. The specific meanings of sex, gender, and sexuality are defined in social interaction and therefore through personal practice. Doing gender and sexuality renders social action accountable in terms of structurally available gender and sexual practices appropriate to one's sex category in the specific social situation in which one acts. It necessarily entails the particular structured gender and sexual relations in specific settings that give behavior its sexed, gendered, and sexual meanings.

In this view, then, although we decide quite early in life that we're a boy or a girl and later we adopt an identity as straight, gay, lesbian, bisexual, etc., the actual everyday "doing" of sex, gender, and sexuality is accomplished systematically and is never a static or a finished product. Rather, people construct sex, gender, and sexuality in specific social situations. In other words, people participate in self-regulating conduct whereby they monitor their own and others' embodied social actions and they respond to and draw from available social structures. This perspective allows for innovation and flexibility in sex, gender, and sexuality construction—and the ongoing potentiality of normative transgression— but also underscores the ever-present possibility of any sexed, gendered, and sexual activity being assessed by copresent interactants. Sex category serves as a resource for the interpretation of situated social conduct, as copresent interactants in each setting attempt to hold accountable behavior as female or male; that is, socially defined membership in one sex category is used as a means of discrediting or accepting gender and sexual practices. Although we construct ourselves as male or female, we situationally embody gender and sexuality according to our own unique experiences, and accountability attempts to maintain *congruence* among sex, gender, and sexuality; that is, male equals masculinity equals sexually desires females and female equals femininity equals sexually desires males.

Moreover, sex, gender, and sexuality construction results from individuals often—but not always—considering the content of their social action and then acting only after internal deliberation about the purpose and consequence of their behavior. *Reflexivity* refers to the capacity to engage in internal conversations with oneself about particular social experiences and then decide how to respond appropriately. In reflexivity we internally mull over specific social events and interactions, we consider how such circumstances make us feel, we prioritize what matters most, and then we plan and decide how to respond (Archer, 2007). Although we internally deliberate and eventually make such reflexive choices to act in particular ways, those choices are based on the situationally socially structured available sex, gender, and sexual practices and discourses. Notwithstanding that sex, gender, and sexuality simply may at specific times be a habitual and routine social practice (Martin, 2003), accountability encourages people to do sex, gender, and sexuality appropriate to particular situations. And accountability and thus reflexivity especially come into play when agents are confronted with a unique social situation—such as a challenge to their sex, gender, or sexuality. Nevertheless, the resulting reflexive social action may not actually have been consciously intended to be a sex, gender, or sexuality practice.

STRUCTURED ACTION

As the forgoing indicates, although sex, gender, and sexuality are "made," so to speak, through the variable unification of internal deliberations and thus reflexive self-regulated practices, these embodied practices do not occur in a vacuum. Instead, they are influenced by the social structural constraints and enablements we experience in particular social situations. *Social structures*, defined as recurring patterns of social phenomena (practices and discourses) that tend to transcend time and space and thus constrain and enable behavior in specific ways, "only exist as the reproduced conduct of situated actors" (Giddens, 1976: 127). In other words, agents draw upon social structures to engage in social action and in turn social structures are (usually) reproduced through that same embodied and accountable social action. In such duality, structure and action are inseparable as knowledgeable human agents of sex, gender, and sexual practices enact social structures by reflexively putting into practice their structured knowledge. Social structures are the "medium" and "outcome" of social action: *medium* because it is through the use of social structures that social action occurs and *outcome* because it is through social action that social structures are reproduced—and sometimes transformed—in time and space (Giddens, 1976; Mouzelis, 2008). Because agents reflexively "do" sex, gender, and sexuality in specific socially structured situations, they reproduce social structures. And given that agents often reproduce sex, gender, and sexual ideals in socially structured specific practices, there are a variety of ways to do them. Within specific social structural settings, particular forms of sex, gender, and sexual practices are available, encouraged, and permitted. Accordingly, sexed, gendered, and sexual *agency* must be viewed as reflexive and embodied structured action—what people, and therefore bodies, do under specific social structural constraints and enablements (Messerschmidt, 1993; 1997; 2000; 2004; 2010; 2012; 2014).

Although there exists a variety of social structures, two are especially salient for conceptualizing sex, gender, and sexuality: relational and discursive. *Relational* social structures establish through social practice the interconnections and interdependence among individuals in particular social settings and thus define social relationships among people in terms of sex, gender, and sexuality. Relational social structures constrain and enable social action. Examples of relational social structures are the informal yet unequal network of sexed, gendered, and sexual "cliques" in elementary and secondary schools and the sex and gender divisions of labor within workplaces. *Discursive* social structures are representations, ideas, and sign systems (language) that produce culturally significant meanings. Discursive social structures establish through social practice regimes or orders of "truth" and what is accepted as "reality" in particular situations. Like relational social structures, discursive social structures constrain and enable the possibilities of social action. Examples of discursive social structures are the notion of "two and only two sexes" mentioned above and social conventions defining styles of dress in terms of sex, gender, and sexuality.

Relational and discursive social structures intersect and work in combination and jointly, but also at times contradictorily. Both relational and discursive social structures are actualized only through particular forms of social action—they have a material base—yet such structured action produces simultaneously particular social relations *and* social meanings that are culturally significant because they shape a sense of what is acceptable and unacceptable behavior for copresent others in specific situations. Through embodied social action individuals produce relational social structures that concurrently proffer meaningful representations (through embodied appearance and practices) for others as a consequence of their social action. And in turn, through embodied social action individuals also produce discursive social structures that concurrently constitute social relations (through representations, ideas, and sign systems) for others as a consequence of their social action. Discursive social structures often are a part of relational social structures and the latter often are a component of the former. The intersection of relational and discursive social structures then constructs the knowledge we use to engage in particular practices—they recursively constrain and enable social action—and it actualizes specific forms of understandings that define what is normal, acceptable, and deviant in particular social situations.

Nevertheless, relational and discursive social structures are not all encompassing and are not always seamlessly accepted by agents without question or objection (Mouzelis, 2008). Through reflexivity agents actually may distance and separate themselves from particular social structures, clearing the path for improvisation and innovation in social action. For example, when confronting social structures, agents at times engage in reflexive internal deliberations and may decide to break from and analyze, investigate, and possibly resist situational structural constraints and enablements (Mouzelis, 2008). As Abby Peterson (2011) shows, it is in reflexivity where we find the mediatory processes whereby structure and action are connected or disconnected. And when such disconnect of agent from structure transpires—and thus *dualism* rather than *duality* occurs—the result often is unique forms of social action. Furthermore, social action may also be influenced by forms of knowledge as *supplemental* constraints and enablements, which are nonrecurring (because they do not transcend time and space) and thus nonstructural. Examples of supplemental constraints and enablements are specific types of social interaction, such as a one-time intimate conversation with a trusted and influential individual as well as our bodies because the body changes over time yet it does situationally constrain and enable social action. In short, sex, gender, and sexual social action emerge from, and are constrained and enabled by, what is always possible within any particular social situation.

POWER

Power is an important structural feature of sex, gender, and sexual relations. Socially structured power relations among men and women are constructed historically on the bases of sex, gender, and sexual preference. In specific contexts some men and some women have greater power than other men or other women; some genders have greater power than other genders; some sexualities have greater power than other sexualities; and the capacity to exercise power and do sex, gender, and sexuality is, for the most part, a reflection of one's place in sex, gender, and sexual structured relations of power. Consequently, in general, heterosexual men and women exercise greater power than do gay men, lesbians, and other sexual minorities; upper-class men and women exercise greater power than do working-class men and women; white men and women exercise greater power than do racial minority men and women; and cisgender people exercise greater power than do transgender people. Power, then, is a relationship that structures social interaction not only between men and women but also among men and among women as well as in terms of gender and sexuality. Nevertheless, power is not absolute and at times may actually shift in relation to different axes of power and powerlessness.

I introduced Raewyn Connell's (1987; 1995) concept of *hegemonic masculinity* in chapter 1 and following Connell's conception I define "hegemonic masculinity" as those masculinities that *legitimate* an unequal *relationship* between men and women, between masculinity and femininity, and among masculinities. The emphasis on *hegemony* and thus legitimation underscores the achievement of hegemonic masculinity through cultural influence and discursive persuasion, encouraging consent and compliance—rather than direct control and commands—to unequal gender relations. Hegemonic masculinities necessarily construct both relational and discursive social structures because they establish relations of sex and gender inequality and at once signify discursively acceptable understandings of sex and gender relations.

In this regard I find that Mimi Schippers' (2007) work (mentioned in chapter 1) is significant because it opens an extremely useful approach of conceptualizing how such *legitimacy* in hegemonic masculinity transpires. Schippers (p. 90) argues that embedded within the meanings of structured gendered relationships are the "qualities members of each gender category should and are assumed to possess"; therefore, it is in "the idealized *quality content* of the categories 'man' and 'woman' that we find the hegemonic significance of masculinity and femininity." For Schippers (p. 91), certain gendered characteristics *legitimate* men's power over women "only when they are symbolically paired with a complementary and inferior quality attached to femininity." The significance of hegemonic forms of masculinity then is found in discursive meanings that legitimate a rationale for structured social relations and that ensure the ascendancy and power of men as well as specific masculinities. What Schippers highlights, therefore, is first the *relationship* between masculinity and femininity and second how a certain masculinity is hegemonic only when it articulates discursively particular *gender qualities* that are *complementary* and *hierarchical* in relation to specific feminine qualities. For example, such a complementary and hierarchical relationship might establish masculinity as constituting physical strength, the ability to use interpersonal violence in the face of conflict, and authority, whereas femininity would embrace physical vulnerability, an inability to use violence effectively, and compliance (p. 91). When both masculine and feminine qualities establish a complementary and hierarchical relationship between them, we have the legitimation of gender hegemony, involving the superordinate position of men and subordinate position of women (p. 94).

Hegemonic masculinities form relational and discursive social structures that have cultural influence but do not determine social action. Hegemonic masculinities often—but not always—underpin the conventions applied in the enactment and reproduction of masculinities (and femininities)—the lived embodied patterns of meanings, which as they are experienced as practice, appear as reciprocally confirming. Hegemonic masculinities relationally and discursively shape a sense of "reality" for men and women in specific situations and are continually renewed, recreated, defended, and modified through social action. And yet they are at times resisted, limited, altered, and challenged. Hegemonic masculinities operate like other social structures as recurring "on-hand" meaningful practices that are culturally influential and thus available to be actualized into social action in a range of different circumstances. They provide a conceptual framework that is materialized in the design of daily practices and interactions. As individuals construct gender hegemony they simultaneously present those relations as culturally significant for others as a consequence of their embodied social action. Power is then constituted through acceptance of and consent to hegemonically masculine forms of knowledge and practice.

In addition to the above, the relationship between hegemonic masculinity and emphasized femininity underpins what has become known as *heteronormativity*, or the legal, cultural, organizational, and interpersonal practices that derive from and reinforce the discursive structure that there are two and only two naturally opposite and complementary sexes (male and female), that gender is a natural manifestation of sex (masculinity and femininity), and that it is natural for the two opposite and complementary sexes to be sexually attracted to each other (heterosexuality). In other words, the social construction of sex differences intersects with the assumption of gender and sexual complementarity, or the notion that men's and women's bodies are naturally compatible and thus "made for each other"—*the* "natural" sex act allegedly involves vaginal penetration by a penis (Jackson and Scott, 2010). Heterosexuality is understood culturally as the natural erotic attraction to sex/gender difference, as well as a natural practice of male active dominance and female passive receptivity, and thus this notion of "natural attraction and practice" reinforces hegemonic masculinity and emphasized femininity as innate, complementary, and hierarchical opposites (Schippers, 2007). Heteronormativity therefore refers to "the myriad ways in which heterosexuality is produced as a natural, unproblematic, taken-for-granted, ordinary phenomenon" (Kitzinger, 2005: 478).

Accordingly, there is nothing "natural" about heterosexuality and indeed the term "heterosexuality" actually did not appear until the 1890s, and then it was used to specifically designate an identity based not on procreation but rather on sexual desire for the opposite sex. Heterosexuality became disconnected from procreation and "normal" sexuality was henceforth defined as heterosexual attraction; "abnormal" sexuality was homosexual attraction. The concept of heterosexuality was defined in terms of its relationship to the concept of homosexuality, both terms categorizing a sexual desire unrelated to procreation, and individuals now began to define their sexual identity according to whether they were attracted to the same or the opposite sex (Seidman, 2010). Steven Seidman (p. 158) articulates well the historically constructed close connection between gender and heterosexuality:

> There can be no norm of heterosexuality, indeed no notion of heterosexuality, without assuming two genders that are coherent as a relationship of opposition and unity. If there were no fixed categories of gender, if there were no "men" and "women," there could be no concept of heterosexuality! So, heterosexuality is anchored by maintaining a gender order through

either celebrating and idealizing gender or by stigmatizing and polluting gender nonconformity.

Gender hegemony and sexual hegemony intersect so that both masculinity and heterosexuality are deemed superior and femininity and homosexuality (and alternative sexualities) are judged to be inferior. The social construction of men and women as naturally different, complementary, and hierarchical sanctions heterosexuality as *the* normal and natural form of sexuality and masculine men and feminine women as *the* normal and natural gender presentation; any sexual or gender construction outside of these dichotomies is considered abnormal. Heteronormativity then reproduces a sexual social structure based on an unequal sexual binary—heterosexuality and homosexuality—that is dependent upon the alleged natural sexual attraction of two and only two opposite and complementary sexes and that in turn constructs heteromasculine and heterofeminine difference. Nevertheless, some heterosexual practices are more powerful than other heterosexual practices; that is, normative heterosexuality determines its own social structure and thus internal boundaries as well as marginalizing and sanctioning sexualities outside those boundaries.

ADDITIONAL MASCULINITIES AND FEMININITIES

In addition to hegemonic masculinity and emphasized femininity, structured action theory identifies additional distinct masculinities and femininities: dominant, dominating, subordinate, and positive. To review (from chapter 1) and add femininities to the theoretical picture, "dominant" masculinities and femininities differ from hegemonic masculinities and emphasized femininities in that they are not always associated with and linked to gender hegemony but refer fundamentally to the most celebrated, common, or current form of masculinity and femininity in a particular social setting (see also Beasley, 2008; 2013). "Dominating" masculinities and femininities are similar to dominant masculinities and femininities but differ in the sense that they involve commanding and controlling specific interactions and exercising power and control over people and events—"calling the shots" and "running the show." Dominant and dominating masculinities and femininities do not necessarily legitimate a hierarchical relationship between men and women, masculinity and femininity. Although hegemonic masculinities and emphasized femininities at times may also be dominant or dominating, dominant and dominating masculinities and femininities are never hegemonic or emphasized if they fail culturally to *legitimate* unequal gender relations; in this latter scenario, dominant and dominating masculinities are thereby constructed *outside* relations of gender hegemony. However, dominant and dominating masculinities and femininities necessarily acquire meaning only in relation to other masculinities and femininities (see Beasley, 2008; 2013; Messerschmidt, 2008; 2010; 2012; 2014).

"Subordinate" masculinities and femininities refer to those masculinities and femininities situationally constructed as lesser than or aberrant and deviant to hegemonic masculinity or emphasized femininity as well as dominant/dominating masculinities and femininities. Depending upon the particular context, such subordination can be conceptualized in terms of, for example, race, class, age, sexualities, or body display/behavior. Given the discussion above, it should be obvious that one of the most significant forms of subordination is that of gay boys/men and lesbian girls/women—the former are culturally feminized and the latter culturally masculinized. In a gender and heteronormative hegemonic culture, then, gayness is socially defined as the embodiment of whatever is expelled from hegemonic masculinity and lesbianism is demarcated as the embodiment of whatever is expelled from

emphasized femininity. Related to this, a second form of subordination usually occurs if there is *incongruence* within sex-gender-
heterosexuality practices. For example, girls and women perceived as female who construct bodily practices defined as masculine, such as expressing sexual desire for girls ("dyke"), acting
sexually promiscuous ("slut"), and/or presenting as authoritarian,
physically aggressive, or take-charge ("bitch") are viewed as polluting "normal" and "natural" hegemonic gender and sexual relations and often are verbally, socially, and physically subordinated
(Schippers, 2007). Similarly, individuals perceived as male but
who construct practices defined as feminine, such as sexually desiring boys or simply practicing celibacy ("fag"), being passive,
compliant, or shy ("sissy"), and/or being physically weak or unad-
venturous ("wimp") likewise are seen as polluting "normal" and
"natural" hegemonic gender and sexual relations and often are
verbally, socially, and physically subordinated (Schippers, 2007).
Social structures that actualize unequal gender and sexual relations then are sustained in part through the subordination of the
above genders and sexualities. Finally, subordination can also occur amongst individuals who construct situationally accountable
masculinities and femininities. For example, the masculinity of a
son may be judged to be subordinate to the masculinity of his
father, and the femininity of a daughter may be considered subordinate to the femininity of her mother. Both of these forms of
subordination occur primarily by reason of age, not because of
any incongruence between sex and gender, and usually are established in relation to dominant/dominating masculinities and femininities and thus practiced independent of gender hegemony.

"Positive" masculinities and femininities are those that actually
may help legitimate an egalitarian relationship between men and
women, between masculinity and femininity, and among masculinities and femininities, and therefore are constructed exterior to
gender hegemonic relational and discursive structures in any par-

ticular setting. Such masculinities and femininities do not assume a normal and natural relationship to sex and sexuality and usually are not constructed as naturally complementary.

Structured action theory permits investigation of the different ways men and women experience their everyday worlds from their particular positions in society and how they relate to other men and women; the embodied sex, gender, and sexual practices are associated with the specific context of individual action and are for the most part self-regulated—through reflexivity—within that context; social actors self-regulate their behavior and make specific reflexive choices in specific socially structured contexts. In this way, then, men and women construct varieties of sex, gender, and sexuality through specific embodied practices. And by emphasizing diversity in sex, gender, and sexual construction, we achieve a more fluid and situated approach to our understanding of embodied sexes, genders, and sexualities.

EMBODIMENT

As I have emphasized, constructing sex, gender, and sexuality entails *embodied* social practices—reflexive structured action. Only through our bodies do we experience the social world, and the very possibility of a social world rests upon our embodiment (Crossley, 2001). As Iris Marion Young (1990: 147–148) long ago pointed out:

> It is the body in its orientation toward and action upon and within its surroundings that constitutes the initial meaning-given act. The body is the first locus of intentionality, as pure presence to the world and openness upon its possibilities. The most primordial intentional act is the motion of the body orienting itself with respect to and moving within its surroundings.

We understand the world from our embodied place in it and our perceptual awareness of situational surrounding space. The body is a sensuous being—it perceives, it touches, and it feels; it is a lived body, and given that consciousness consists of perceptual sensations, it is therefore part of the body and not a separate substance (Crossley, 2001). The mind and the body are inseparably linked—a binary divide is a fiction—and live together as one in the social construction of sex, gender, and sexuality. In this conceptualization, then, the body forms the whole of our being and, therefore, one's reflexive sexed, gendered, and sexual self is located in the body, which in turn acts, and is acted upon, within a social environment. And in contemporary industrialized societies the body is central to the social construction of self (Giddens, 1991). A proficient and able body is necessary for social action and, therefore, embodied discipline is fundamental to the competent social agent: "It is integral to the very nature both of agency and of being accepted (trusted) by others as competent" (p. 100).

Related to the above is Pat Martin's (2003) differentiation between "gender practices" and "practicing gender." The term "gender practices" refers to forms of embodied behavior that are structurally "available" in specific social settings for individuals "to enact in an encounter or situation in accord with (or in violation of) the gender institution" (p. 354). In other words, these are potential, situationally available embodied structured actions "that people know about and have the capacity or agency to do, assert, perform, or mobilize" (p. 354). The term "practicing gender" entails actually "doing" the situationally available embodied sexed, gender, and sexual practices and is usually accomplished with copresent interactants and usually reflexively. To do gender reflexively individuals must "carefully consider the content of one's actions and act only after careful consideration of the intent, content, and effects of one's behavior" (p. 356). Although we make reflexive choices to act in particular ways, that reflexivity is based on the situationally embodied gender practices associated with contextual relational and discursive social structures.

Through embodied structured action individuals "do" sex, gender, and sexuality while simultaneously reproducing structures and presenting such practices as resources for others as a consequence of their embodiment. The social situations in which embodied actions are oriented "are populated by others and it is these others, in part, towards whom the actions are oriented. Action is other oriented" (Crossley, 1995: 141). Embodied social action is embedded within the specific social structural context of the agent, so that what we actually conceptualize are social situations that require specific "practical accommodation from our action" (p. 136)—we reflexively respect, acknowledge, reproduce, and sometimes resist structured embodied practices. And as Goffman (1979: 6) acutely observes, such embodied actions are situational forms of "social portraiture" in which individuals discursively convey information that "the others in the gathering will need in order to manage their own courses of action—which knowledgeability he [sic] in turn must count on in carrying out his [sic] own designs." Doing sex, gender, and sexuality therefore is necessarily both reflexive and physical; it is intelligent, meaningful, structured, and embodied.

Bodies are active in the production and transmission of social structures as well as embodied social actions, and are based on the reaction of others to our embodiment—whether or not it is judged accountable is important to our sense of self. Embodied accountability is vital to an individual's situational recognition as a competent sexed, gendered, and sexual social agent. If an individual's embodied appearance and practice is categorized by others as "failed," that degradation may result in a spoiled self-concept and identity (Goffman, 1968). Consequently, adequate participation in social life depends upon the successful presenting, monitoring, and interpreting of bodies.

Goffman helps us understand how doing sex, gender, and sexuality are socially structured in the sense that we accomplish all
three bodily and in a manner that is accountable to situationally
populated others. Individuals exhibit embodied sex, gender, and
sexual competence through their appearance and by producing
situationally appropriate "behavioral styles" that respond properly
to the styles produced by others. In other words, "competent"
individuals develop an embodied capacity to provide and to read
structured discursive depictions of sex, gender, and sexuality in
particular settings, and appropriate body management is crucial
to the smooth flow of interaction essential to satisfactory attribution and accountability by others. To be "read" by others as male,
female, masculine, feminine, straight, gay, lesbian, etc., individuals must ensure that their proffered selves are maintained
through situationally appropriate display and behavior—the body
is social and social settings are created through intercorporeality.

But in addition, properly accountable bodies construct relational and discursive social structures and they signal and facilitate through their appearance and action the maintenance of sex,
gender, and sexual power dynamics. To be sure, suitably adorned
and comported bodies constitute the "shadow and the substance"
of unequal sex, gender, and sexual structures (Goffman, 1979: 6):
"The expression of subordination and domination through the
swarm of situational means is more than a mere tracing of symbol
or ritualistic affirmation of social hierarchy. These expressions
considerably constitute the hierarchy; they are the shadow and
the substance." Individuals produce (and at times challenge) socially structured sex, gender, and sexual relations through their
embodied appearance and actions.

The body is an essential part of sex, gender, and sexual construction in which we fashion appearance and actions to create
properly and situationally adorned and performed bodies. The
body is an inescapable and integral part of doing sex, gender, and

sexuality, entailing social practice that constantly refers to bodies and what bodies do; it is not social practice reduced to the body (Connell, 2000). Constructing sex, gender, and sexuality involves a dialectical relationship in which practice deals with the biological characteristics of bodies: "It gives them a social determination. The connection between social and natural structures is one of practical relevance, not causation" (Connell, 1987: 78). In the social construction of sex, gender, and sexuality bodily similarities between men and women are negated and suppressed, whereas bodily differences are exaggerated. Indeed, the body is essential to, for example, the discourse of "two and only two sexes" in the sense that "men have penises and women do not." The body is significant for our fundamental sex, gender, and sexual projects discussed above, our sense of sex, gender, and sexual self that we reflexively sustain through time and space. Bodies impact our recurring self-attributions and thus one's identity as male or female, masculine or feminine, and straight or gay. Because "sex" is associated with genitalia there is likely to be a degree of social standardization of individual lives—we recursively construct ourselves as, for example, a "boy/man" or as a "girl/woman" with a particular sexual orientation and thus such identities constrain and enable our social action. For most people sex is the primary claimed identity that is relatively solid, unchanging, and taken-for-granted while gender and sexuality are qualifiers to the previously assumed sex (Paechter, 2006). Nevertheless, some turn this on its head—such as certain transgender people—whereby sex is the qualifier and gender is the primary mode in which one relates to the world (p. 259).

Bodies participate in social action by delineating courses of social conduct: bodies are agents of social practice and, given the context, will do certain things and not others; our bodies are *supplemental* constraints and enablers of social action and therefore they situationally mediate and influence social practices (Connell,

1995). The body often is lived in terms of what it can "do" and the "consequence of bodily practice is historicity: the creation and transformation of situations. Bodies are drawn into history and history is constituted through bodies" (Connell, 1998: 7). In short, the body is a participant in the shaping and generating of social practice and it is impossible to consider human agency without taking sexed, gendered, and sexual embodiment into account.

CHALLENGES

Nevertheless, certain occasions present themselves as more effectively intimidating for demonstrating and affirming embodied sex, gender, and sexuality. In certain situations individuals may experience body betrayal and be identified by others as embodying sex, gender, or sexual "failure." The constitution of sex, gender, and sexuality through bodily appearance and performance means that sex, gender, and sexual accountability are vulnerable when the situationally and socially structured appropriate appearance and performance are not (for whatever reason) sustained. Because the taken-for-granted sex, gender, and sexuality of individuals can be challenged in certain contexts, each may become particularly salient. They are, as David Morgan (1992: 47) would put it, "more or less explicitly put on the line," and the responding social action can generate an intensified reflexivity and a distinct type of sex, gender, or sexual construction. Such challenges are contextually embodied interactions that result in sex, gender, or sexual degradation—the individual is constructed as a sexed, gendered, or sexually "deviant" member of society. Such challenges arise from interactional threats and insults from peers, teachers, parents, or workmates and from situationally and bodily defined sex, gender, and sexual expectations that are not achievable. Such challenges, in various ways, proclaim a man or boy or a woman or girl subordinate in contextually defined embodied terms. Sex, gender, and sexual challenges may motivate social action toward specific situationally embodied practices that attempt to correct the subordinating social situation (Messerschmidt 1993; 1997; 2000; 2004; 2010; 2012; 2014). Given that such interactions question, undermine, and/or threaten one's sex, gender, or sexuality, only contextually "appropriate" sex, gender, and sexual embodied practices can help overcome the challenge. The existence of sex, gender, and sexual challenges alerts us to the transitory and fleeting nature of sex, gender, and sexual construction and to how particular forms of social action may arise as sexed, gendered, or sexual practices when they are regularly threatened and contested.

Social action is never simply an autonomous event but is amalgamated into larger assemblages—what is labeled here as socially structured embodied actions. The socially structured situational ideals of sex, gender, and sexuality encourage specific lines of social action, and relational and discursive social structures shape the capacities from which sex, gender, and sexuality actions are constructed over time. Men and boys and women and girls negotiate the situations that face them in everyday life and in the process pursue a sex, gender, and sexuality project. From this perspective, then, social action is often—but not always—designed with an eye to one's sex, gender, and sexual accountability individually, bodily, situationally, and structurally. Structured action theory, then, permits us to explore how and in what respects sex, gender, and sexual embodied practices are constituted in certain settings at certain times. In short, to understand masculinities, we must appreciate how structure and action are woven inextricably into the ongoing reflexive activities of "doing" embodied sex, gender, and sexual practices.

Let us now turn to the application of structured action theory (in chapters 3, 4, and 5) to the data generated in the life-history interview and content analysis studies outlined in the introduction.

3

WIMPS: SAM AND JERRY

As pointed out in the introduction, chapter 3 focuses on two white working-class teenage boys from New England—Sam and Jerry (both pseudonyms)—and their specific constructions of masculinities. I begin this chapter with Sam.

SAM

Sam was a short, overweight, boyish-looking eighteen-year-old with short blond hair who was markedly animated while articulating his life story. He wore a bright-blue youth-prison "jumpsuit" with "slippers" on his feet to both interviews, and he was so excited about telling me his story that he came to the interviews with detailed lists of important episodes and circumstances in his life. He also pointed out at several stages of our conversations that the interviews helped him understand the past and that he hoped his story would help others. Sam was incarcerated for sexual violence against two young girls. In what follows, I describe through Sam's words his different gender constructions.

A Localized Subordinate Masculinity

Sam was from a working-class suburb where he lived with his two adoptive parents and younger biological sister. Like other members of the "respectable" working class, the family owned its own home when Sam was growing up. Sam became a member of this family when he and his sister were abandoned by their biological mother.

Sam and his sister were assigned to a variety of foster homes, eventually being adopted when Sam was five by his current foster parents. When Sam was younger his "mom" and "dad" (what he calls them) worked at a service industry job and a skilled manual job, respectively, generating a modest working-class income. Sam's mother did all the cooking at home as well as the shopping for food and other necessities. The kids helped their mother with daily household cleaning. Their father, according to Sam, "mowed the lawn, loafed around, and worked with his tools."

Sam thus grew up among and successfully participated in explicit relational and discursive socially structured practices defining "men's work" and "women's work" at home and in the workplace—Sam reflexively drew on these structures and it was through interaction at home that he accordingly came to understand himself as "a boy." Further, these overlapping social structures nourished Sam's idea of future labor-force participation: Sam saw himself as a male and reflexively decided that he wanted to "work with tools" after finishing high school. And by the time he was in high school Sam had his own automobile that was just as "decked out as Dad's."

Sam reported substantial family cohesiveness and stability, describing very close contact with both parents: "We went on many vacations together as a family—going camping, fishing, and hunting. We had a great time together." Sam indicated that he experienced an especially warm and affectionate family relationship (discipline was verbal, not physical) and remembered specifically bonding with his father: "He taught me all about tools and everything else, and I used to be able to hand him the tools when he was working on trailer trucks." Moreover, Sam's father had the power in the home: "Dad was the one who kept in control over everything." Sam's mother and the kids always yielded to his dad's decisions: "We always looked to Dad; he was the one who took control." Sam's father then embodied a localized hegemonic masculinity and Sam's mother emphasized femininity, and these structured gender relations had a major discursive impact on Sam.

Sam obviously identified with his father, who was his initial model for developing a specific type of masculinity. When I asked Sam if he was concerned about having approval from his father, he stated, "Yeah, that meant a lot to me, Dad telling me I did a good job helping him." Although Sam's father constructed a hegemonic masculinity in relation to his mother's emphasized femininity, in relation to Sam he practiced a dominating masculinity. Sam's interviews clearly show that within the family a substantial commitment toward, and a smooth reproduction of, a subordinate masculinity was constructed by Sam in relation to his father's dominating masculinity, and Sam's accountable subordinate masculinity included numerous practices such as working with tools, fishing and hunting, and manual labor. Sam used the relational and discursive social structures at home to engage in masculine social action, in turn he reproduced these social structures through his particular social action and therefore duality of structure and action transpired. Sam expanded his conception of masculinity at the time in the following way: "Success at work, power, money, strong, being like Dad." Sam never was the victim of violence at home nor did he ever engage in assaultive or sexual violence *against family members*. And it was in this setting where Sam initially took up a fundamental project of masculinity as his own—he clearly identified as a boy who embodied localized (sub-

ordinate) masculine appearance and practices in this social structural setting—and there was congruence between his sex category
and gender behavior in this milieu.

A Localized Femininity

At school Sam collided with an unsettling social situation maintaining differing social structures. In elementary school after
breaking away from a group of "troublemakers," Sam was subjected to consistent verbal bullying by the dominant popular boys
because of his physical size and shape (he was shorter and heavier
than the other boys), eventually to the extent of "living in fear of
going to school." Sam did not do well in school because, according to him, he internally worried more about being verbally bullied than doing schoolwork and was placed in special education
courses. During his eighth-grade year his classmates were recalled as making the following remark: "Everybody looked at me
like 'Oh, there is something wrong with him.'"

Being verbally bullied about shortness and obesity and feeling
rejection for being "slow" intellectually extended through eighth
grade and into high school. Although Sam observed numerous
instances of boys fighting at school because of bullying, he reflexively decided not to respond directly to the bullies because of his
physical size—he did not want to be "beat up." As a result, Sam
constantly watched his back, watched where he was stepping,
"always really nervous at school, because people picked on me."
When asked if he discussed the bullying with his parents, Sam
replied:

> Yeah, I talked to my dad about it. My dad kept telling me to
> fight back, let them know I was a tough guy. He would tell me:
> "Hit them right back. Don't let them get to you, don't let them
> bug you." And I wanted to fight back but I didn't feel like I was
> strong, like I could fight back like dad said.

Sam reflexively mulled over the in-school relational and discursive social structures negatively impacting him as well as the ongoing embarrassment in school for poor grades and for being a "special ed kid." Momentarily distancing himself from the structures—and thus dualism between structure and action now appears—in order to decide what to do, Sam primarily had internal conversations about bodily inadequacy because of his physical size and shape, as well as a sense of powerlessness for his inability to fight back as his father recommended and as his peers expected. Sam therefore internally deliberated about two particular yet contradictory supplemental constraints and enablements—his *body* as a hindrance in his ability to "fight back" and his *conversation* with "dad" suggesting he do so. In the end and to avoid further assessment of his conduct by the bullies, Sam decided to become a loner at school and he chose to stop discussing the bullying with his father because he did not want to disappoint him. And Sam did all he could to avoid any interaction with the bullies at school. As he states:

> They would call me "porky," a "wimp," that I couldn't stick up for myself, that I was a "mama's boy." I wasn't worth anything according to them. I felt like I was a girl, someone they [the dominant popular boys] shouldn't hang around or talk to. So, of course I didn't tell Dad, and my loner lifestyle.

The boys who bullied Sam were "the popular ones," dominant boys who played sports, attended parties, participated in heterosexuality, and had lots of friends; they represented the most celebrated form of masculinity in Sam's school. When I asked Sam how they identified him as a "wimp," he replied that they would "try to get me to fight with them. They would say, 'Come on fat boy, fight.' But they were all tall and strong so I'd run away. I wouldn't stay around them. And they'd call me names."

Sam is revealing here the institutionalization of masculine relations in his school—the informal "clique" relational and discursive social structures (dominant versus wimp). Sam is telling us about the policing of masculinities embedded in these structured relations whereby certain boys are subordinated, and Sam is one of those boys. He is positioned as subordinate without his own volition and effort; it results more from his inactivity than from his activity. And as the bullying continues Sam eventually is feminized through comments made about his inability to "fight back," about his nonmuscular "fat" and "wimpish" body, and about his complete lack of participation in sports; as Sam states in the quote above: "I felt like I was a girl." Sam's feminized relational and discursive position then is underpinned by his interactional uncoupling with the embodied masculinities associated with these structures, such as fighting back when bullied, participating in sports, and possessing a muscular body. Sam was unable to link or fuse himself with these masculine practices in any way. Indeed, we "see" Sam negotiating the relational and discursive social structures at school yet he is unable to become a practicing member of these structures which then results in his subordinate and feminized position. Through bullying then Sam is constructed as a hybridized "feminine boy."

The dominant-subordinate relationship between the bullies and Sam furthermore transmutes into a localized in-school *dominating* form of hegemonic masculinity in which the popular dominant bullies embodied aggressiveness, invulnerability, and the capacity to engage in physical violence while Sam embodies passivity, vulnerability, and the inability to engage in physical violence, both sets of gendered qualities situationally associated with masculinity and femininity respectively. Unequal masculine and feminine relations were therefore constituted within the in-school masculine social structures and were established in and through exclusively assigned male bodies. By means of verbal bullying, then, Sam was invested with situationally defined "inferior" gendered qualities that assimilated with femininity while the bullies were invested with situationally defined "superior" qualities that assimilated with masculinity. Moreover, the bullies were commanding and controlling the interaction, they were exercising power and control over Sam, they were "calling the shots" and "running the show." We therefore have the cultural ascendancy of an in-school localized dominating hegemonic masculine and emphasized feminine relationship that simultaneously circulates a legitimating discursive justification for gender inequality. A fleeting dominating hegemonic masculinity was established through the bullies-Sam relationship because Sam was both subordinated and feminized during these interactions and a dominating relationship was established. Accordingly, Sam did not have any friends at school: "I wasn't like one of them; I wasn't one that had friends to hang out with." In short, Sam found himself in an unaccountable masculine position at school and was constructed as feminine because according to the bullies there existed incongruence between Sam's perceived sex category and his gender behavior.

Sam clearly was reflexively questioning his ability to protect himself from the ongoing "degradation ceremonies" at school, unable to control such a threatening environment and thus unable to be masculine like the other boys. In fact, he internally viewed himself as incapable of making the "appropriate" masculine response—fighting back physically—which he had learned through interaction at school and from his special mentor (father). And significantly, he reflexively decided he could not discuss this situation with his parents because he determined that he would "let them down" for not being able to handle the situation as his father instructed. By the time he was fifteen years old Sam's masculinity was seriously challenged—he lacked masculine resources and therefore reflexively he felt extremely powerless, distressed, and subordinate at school—Sam was unable to accountably construct either a dominant or a hegemonic masculinity and instead he was seriously subordinated and femininized in this setting.

During his freshman year in high school Sam began to develop internal conversations consisting of sexually objectifying and desiring girls. He learned to objectify and desire girls from interaction at school and not from his parents. As Sam states: "Kids were talking at school about 'blow jobs,' 'getting laid,' telling dirty jokes, and about having sex and stuff like that." Sam constantly heard the dominant popular boys' "sex talk" about sexual objectification of girls as well as heterosexual exploits and experiences. He reflexively desired to participate in heterosexuality but he concluded that because he was a loner he could not meet any girls his age and he could therefore not share the "sex-talk" camaraderie. It was this culturally ascendant heterosexual social structure practiced in the form of schoolboy discursive chat, then, that was Sam's initial source of information about sexuality and thus his sexual awakening—in this setting Sam reflexively wanted to affix a heterosexual project to his ongoing attempt at masculine construction. Here Sam is drawing on the in-school heterosexual "sex talk" among boys, a socially structured and culturally influential discourse at school that emphasizes the relationship between dominant masculinity and heterosexual objectification and exploits. It was during his freshman year, then, that Sam became very interested in heterosexuality: reflexively he decided that he also wanted to experience heterosexual relations so as to "learn what it was like." Clearly, this development had its gender component. When asked why he eventually decided that he wanted to experience sexuality, Sam added, "I thought, well, I'm a guy, so this is something that every guy does, that I want to be part of this. I want to be like the other guys. I want to know what it feels like, I want to know what goes on."

Sam is actualizing his internal self-attribution as a male—he identifies as "a guy" and thus for Sam the practice of heterosexuality is in part what people with assigned male bodies do with those bodies. Sam knew several girls at school with whom he wished to have a sexual relationship, but because of the constant bullying, "I didn't think I was good enough. I didn't have the trust enough to gain access to a girl. I didn't think any girl would be interested in me." Sam reflexively objectified girls and wanted to develop sexual contact with girls in order to be "like the other guys" and to satisfy his self-attribution as "a guy," but through his internal conversations he determined that he was unable to fulfill this situationally defined dominant masculine criterion—Sam is incapable of constructing dominant or hegemonic heteromasculinity and therefore his masculinity was seriously challenged in this setting.

By age fifteen, then, Sam was experiencing degradation ceremonies at school about his physical size and shape, as well as earning poor grades. His inability to "fight back" internally haunted him and significantly added to his lack of masculine resources and accompanying negative masculine self-esteem. This masculine insecurity was further enhanced by his inability to be a "real man" through developing the intensely sought after sexual relationships with girls his age. Sam found himself in the position of being unable to actualize and thus construct any of the social structural masculine expectations at school.

A Localized Dominating Masculinity

Accordingly, Sam reflexively decided to attempt to overcome his lack of masculine resources and thereby diminish the negative masculine feelings and situations through controlling and manipulating behaviors involving the use of sexual power. Sam chose to turn to a specific form of masculine behavior that was available to him—expressing sexual control and power over younger girls.

During his freshman year in high school Sam began babysitting a few neighborhood girls (6–8 years old) in his house after school and then all day during the summer. It was Sam's idea to babysit and his parents instantly accepted, believing it was a splendid decision on Sam's part. During this year in high school—a time when he experienced most of the distressing events discussed earlier and when he "discovered" heterosexuality—Sam reflexively decided that one way he could be a "real guy" is by sexually assaulting some of the girls he babysat:

> I wanted to have some kind of sexual experience. And that didn't happen at school. I mean, I wasn't around other people, I didn't experience relationships with people my own age. And I started seeing the girls I babysat as being innocent and being able to take advantage of easily. I looked at how my life was, how I feared the people at school, so I figured I could get a girl I was babysitting easier. That's why I wanted to babysit.

The adults trusted Sam with the girls because in front of them he had, through his internal conversations, initially decided to be gentle and caring toward them. The girls liked Sam and thus he reflexively determined ways to gain their trust and becoming a babysitter was a major turning point in Sam's life. As he interprets it: "Babysitting gave me a place where I was in control because I was taking care of kids and I had control over them." When asked how he chose specific girls to abuse, Sam explained that he noticed some of the girls were "more quiet" and more vulnerable and therefore more easily exploitable.

Sam manipulated two of the girls into fondling him and performing oral sex on him for two years, reflexively deliberating about and deciding how to use specific strategies to gain access to them: "I kept gaining ways to manipulate, ways to like bribe, like act like I was helping them, act like I was doing good things for them, like playing games with them. For example, 'I'll play [computer games] with you if you do this for me.'" Sam stated that he chose not to blatantly physically threaten the girls he sexually assaulted. Instead, he reflexively decided to "wrestle with them and throw them around, and pretend that I know all this self-defense stuff, making it look like I was invincible, like I was strong, tough, and couldn't be hurt. That they couldn't fight back. Through that, that's what I used to scare them."

The following extended dialogue reveals what the sexual violence accomplished for Sam:

Q. How did it make you feel when you were able to manipulate the girls you were babysitting?

A. I was getting away with something that nobody else that I saw was getting away with. I felt that I was number one. I felt like I was better, like I was a better person, because I could play this little game with them and they didn't see what was going on. Like, I could trap 'em. It was like then they really didn't have much of a choice but to go along with what I wanted them to do.

Q. You felt special?

A. Yeah, because it was like I could manipulate anybody, because it was like I could put on a facade like as if I was a good person all the time. I would be such a nice person. I went to church, I did things for people, I acted nice. I would paint the image like I was a good boy. And all the while I was having sex with these girls.

Q. How did it make you feel when you sexually assaulted these two girls?

A. I didn't feel like I was small anymore, because in my own grade, my own school, with people my own age, I felt like I was a wimp, the person that wasn't worth anything. But when I did this to the girls, I felt like I was big, I was in control of everything.

Q. And you continued to sexually assault these girls?

A. Yes, that's why I kept doing it, 'cause I felt that control and I wanted that control more and more and more. And that's why it was hard for me to stop, because I'd have to return to that old me of being small and not being anything. I wasn't good at sports, and tough and strong and stuff, so I wasn't fitting in with anybody that was really popular. I was like a small person, someone that nobody really paid attention to. I was the doormat at school. People walked all over me and I couldn't fight back.

Q. Did you feel you were entitled to these girls?

A. I felt like I should be able to have sexual contact with anybody that I wanted to. And I couldn't do that with girls my own age. So I felt like, okay, I'll get it from the girls I was babysitting.

Q. Why did you feel entitled to sex?

A. Like, well, I'm a guy. I'm supposed to have sex. I'm supposed to be like every other guy. And so I'm like them, but I'm even better than them [dominant popular boys], because I can manipulate. They don't get the power and the excitement. They have a sexual relationship with a girl. She can say what she wants and she has the choice. But the girls I babysat didn't have the choice. It was like I made it look like they had a choice, but when they stated their choice, if they said no, I like bugged them and bugged them until they didn't say no.

Q. How did that make you feel in relation to the other males at school?

A. I was like better than every other guy, because there was no way I could get rejected. It was like, okay, they can have their relationships, I'm gonna do whatever I want. I'm better than they are.

Drawing on the in-school culturally influential dominating hegemonically relational and discursive masculine social structures, the dominant relational and discursive heterosexual social structures, and his self-attribution as "a guy," Sam reflexively decides to practice sexual violence to solve his masculine dilemma. And through this sexual violence, Sam actually constructed a localized *dominating* masculinity—not a localized hegemonic masculinity—in relation to the girls he sexually assaulted. The violent interaction did indeed produce an unequal masculine/feminine relationship. The gender effects of Sam's sexual violence inscribe the girls who embody weakness and vulnerability as feminine and Sam who embodies strength and invulnerability as masculine, thus constructing "inferior" emphasized feminine survivors and a "superior" hegemonic masculine perpetrator. However, these unequal relations were confined to the basement of Sam's house and therefore lacked cultural ascendancy and accordingly any legitimating influence. Thus, while Sam was *complicit* with hegemonic masculinity he actually did not construct hegemony. Yet simultaneously Sam is commanding and controlling the violent interaction, he is exercising aggressive and dominating interpersonal power over the girls and the situation: he is "calling the shots" and "running the show." Sam is thus constructing a dominating masculinity through sexual violence and now *for him* congruence among sex and gender is established; indeed, in his mind Sam is no longer a wimp or a hybridized feminine boy but rather he is supermasculine.

JERRY

Jerry was a tall, slightly overweight seventeen-year-old who displayed considerable maturity and self-reliance. He had short dark hair, a plump cute face, and he wore a button-down long-sleeve shirt, baggy jeans, and tennis shoes to both interviews. Jerry presented the relaxed deportment of a happy and at-ease individual who engaged easily in conversation with an adult; we seemingly could have discussed his life for days. In what follows, I describe through Jerry's words his different gender constructions.

A Localized Positive Masculinity

Jerry lives in a small house located in the center of a working-class town. His earliest memory is living alone with his mother who had separated from his father because of his alcohol abuse. To make ends meet, Jerry's mother worked two jobs in the unskilled-labor market. Early on Jerry felt very close to his mother. Although she worked a lot, he was proud of the fact that "she managed to keep things together for us."

While his mother worked Jerry was cared for by several different couples who were friends of the family. Depending on the day of the week and the time of day, Jerry would stay with one or another of the couples. Although he rotated among "babysitting" families, he has only fond memories of the many adults who cared for him: "They were all great. I had a lot of fun with all of them."

Around the age of six Jerry met his biological father for the first time. He explained to me how this meeting emerged:

I had always asked, "Hey, where is Dad?" 'cause I always saw these kids with their dad. My mom is always really honest with me. That's the way we've always been, really straightforward with each other. She told me that he was a recovering alcoholic and that maybe someday I'd see him. Finally she called my grandfather and found out where my dad was, and called him, and they set up a thing where he came over to the house.

Jerry thought it was "really cool" when he first met his father because they had a wonderful time together; they went for a walk in the park and spent the entire afternoon side by side as one. Before Jerry's father left that day "we made plans to get back together soon." And it was not long after this first meeting with his father that Jerry's parents actually reconciled and all three began living under the same roof. This was exciting to Jerry because now he was like the other kids—he had both a mother and a father, and he loved his father immensely.

Jerry's father owned a small business in the unskilled manual-labor market and "worked very hard at it." He worked full-time during the day and was extremely tired when he came home in the afternoon. Nevertheless, "we'd play games and watch TV and stuff like that. He'd take me places and we'd just hang out together." When I asked Jerry who his heroes were when he was in elementary school, he stated:

My dad for one of them because he did really hard work and everything. So that made me pretty proud of him. I always respected people that did hard work—my grandfather, great grandfather, those kinds of folks.

Q. What was it about hard work that impressed you?

A. Well, when you've finished hard work it really shows that you have done something.

Q. Did that have a masculine image to you?

A. Not really, because my mom worked hard at two jobs and I knew she was working hard to keep the family up.

Q. What did you want to be when you grew up?

A. I wanted to be like my dad and mom: a hard worker at something I liked to do.

This closeness with his father in particular nourished Jerry's idea of future labor-force participation: Jerry drew from the relational and discursive socially structured practices at home that emphasized the binary construction of sex and he thus saw himself as one side of that binary—a boy—who wants to have a similar business after finishing high school and work hard at it. "If I start my business right out of school and I do it smart, by learning from dad's mistakes that he's made, I can go on to have a wicked business." Drawing from the relational and discursive social structures at home Jerry maps out a future work plan for himself.

Jerry was also extremely pleased and proud that his father overcame addiction to alcohol. The two were so close that Jerry would attend the "alcohol rehab" meetings with his father, and then the two would talk after each meeting. Jerry has affectionate memories not only of his father speaking up at the meetings but also of the special talks afterward. In particular, his father always expressed to Jerry during these conversations that it was not Jerry's fault that he became an alcoholic—Jerry's father took full responsibility for his addiction. Because Jerry's father was contributing economically to the household his mother was able to quit one of her two jobs and had time to pursue other interests (for example, she enrolled part-time at a local university where she took classes now and then, based on personal interests).

Despite these positive developments, Jerry's parents seemed unable to get along with each other. Their difficulties were not related to his father's past problems with alcohol—he remained alcohol-free—or his mother's attending university. Rather, their problems centered on financial issues and consisted of verbal battles—never any physical violence—between the two. Jerry discussed with both parents the issues involved and the nature of the arguments; they consistently stated that the arguments were not Jerry's fault but only reflected an inability to work out financial matters. "There never was anything negative towards me from my parents, always positive things." Although these arguments constituted one of the most distressing events in Jerry's family life, his parents always protected Jerry from responsibility for their problems. In fact, Jerry and his parents were very "connected." Jerry experienced a warm and affectionate relationship with both. "We did everything together. We'd go cross-country skiing, we'd go camping, go on hikes—we were quite an outdoor family." Jerry went hunting and fishing with his dad, helped his mom and dad in the kitchen, and helped his mom in the garden. "I always liked being in the kitchen" and "there was this wonderful garden that me and my mom would be in together." Jerry then grew up among, drew from, and successfully actualized through his in-home social actions the gender egalitarian relational and discursive social structures at home.

When Jerry was in elementary school and junior high school, he was responsible for some of the household chores such as emptying the garbage, getting wood, feeding the pets, setting the table, cutting the lawn, and helping with the cooking and cleaning. Both parents worked together to cook the evening meal. Jerry remembers especially that sometimes "I'd get home from school and I could smell just-baked pies as I walked up the driveway. There would like be three pies on the table that my dad baked. And I'd be like, oh yeah!" Although his father worked at a "masculine" job and his mother at a "feminine" job, at home Jerry observed and participated in both "masculine" and "feminine" forms of domestic labor. Nevertheless, Jerry never particularly liked chores, and frequently performed them in a "real half-ass way." Although his parents would be upset with him for his performance of these duties, he was never disciplined harshly. "They would never send me to my room or anything like that. They'd take stuff away, you know . . . or they'd threaten me that I couldn't do certain stuff on weekends." Jerry was never spanked by either parent; indeed, he never felt subordinate to his parents. Although he clearly identified with his father, Jerry's mother also had a major influence on him. His parents' equal participation in household labor—as well as their renunciation of interpersonal physical violence—constructed relational and discursive social structures that defined for him both an alternative relationship and a form of masculinity that differed from the hegemonic and dominating models practiced by Sam's father. Jerry's father and mother respectively embodied a localized positive masculinity and femininity and Jerry seemed to adopt what was offered. Jerry turned to the gender equal social structures at home to engage in social action and he in turn reproduced these social structures (albeit sometimes in a "real half-ass way") through this same social action. And it is in this setting where Jerry began to take up a project of this type of masculinity as his own; his fundamental gender project was to be like "Dad." Jerry clearly identified as a boy who embodied an accountably nonviolent positive masculinity through both his sex appearance and his gender practices and thus at home the duality of structure and action was prevalent.

A Localized Dominant Masculinity

For Jerry school was not as congenial a place as home. He was an average student and from elementary school on through high school Jerry was the target of the dominant popular boys' consistent verbal bullying for being overweight. "I was called 'chubby' and 'fat ass' a lot. I was laughed at, pushed around, and it would really drag me down." Like Sam, then, Jerry found himself confronting a new combined relational and discursive social structure at school and Jerry reflexively responded by internally mulling over the bullying by the popular dominant boys at school. Ultimately Jerry decided to avoid interacting in public as much as possible because actually he accepted the characterization of his body by the popular dominant boys: "I didn't like going out in public because I felt small and insecure. I was average height but fat. I did a lot of stuff by myself and didn't go out a lot."

Q. You were very concerned about the way you looked?

A. Well, as a kid you're always concerned about your physical looks. And I was very concerned about how people saw me and the way I saw myself.

Q. Can you expand on that a little for me?

A. Oh, just really low self-esteem, just a bad self-image of myself. I didn't like myself if that's the way other people saw me. I was big outside but I felt small inside.

Like Sam, Jerry is revealing for us the institutionalization of masculine structured relations in his school—the informal "clique" relational and discursive social structures—and his reflexive response. Jerry is positioned in a subordinate relationship to the dominant boys through verbal bullying about the size and shape of his body. And like Sam, he is placed in this masculine subordinate position without his own choice or purposeful undertaking but rather exclusively through the discursive practices of the dominant popular boys. However, Jerry reflexively deliberates about his positioning in these social structures and decides simply to refrain as much as possible from being seen in public.

Notwithstanding, Jerry was unable to escape the negative impact these structures imposed on him and he continued to internally develop the same reflexive response: Jerry developed a painful lack of masculine self-esteem at school because of the acute distress over the verbal bullying and subordinating comments about his body. Consequently in third grade—after further reflexivity—he decided to draw on the acceptable masculine practice in the school to "fight back" when bullied and accordingly Jerry became involved in a number of "fistfights" at school. These fights were simply part of what Jerry labeled "playground business," which he defined as "some kid does something and the other kid takes it as he has insulted him, so he goes up and hits the kid for insulting him. That's how kids in my grade school handled business on the playground." The bullying by the dominant boys compelled Jerry to internally feel subordinate, insecure, and small at school. So during his internal deliberations about this masculine insecurity he decided he would respond according to the playground practice of appropriately handling "playground business." "Kids would bully me and then I'd feel better by bullying other kids. If I got bullied, then I had to put someone down by beating the shit out of him." If Jerry did not bully or fight back, he would be called a wimp: "Kids would keep bullying me." Jerry reflexively decided that he wanted to be "tough" in front of the other kids, so he got into eight fights that year. The following dialogue further develops how Jerry consented to, became complicit with, and reproduced these particular relational and discursive social structures through his violent practices:

Q. Did you fight back against the kids who bullied you?

A. Yeah, sometimes, and sometimes I'd go after other kids.

Q. How did that make you feel?

A. It made me feel that if I could bring somebody else down, then I would be higher than them and that was better.

Q. You beat up some kids?

A. Oh, yeah. I lost some and won some.

Like Sam, then, the verbal bullying constructed a gender challenge for Jerry as he was now defined as subordinate in relation to the popular dominant bullies. And Jerry reflexively decided to respond in a way that the particular culturally ascendant relational and discursive social structures of the school emphasized—that is, with physical violence—which initially negated the subordination and allowed Jerry to construct an in-school *dominant* masculinity. Through reflexivity, then, Jerry decided to use these social structures at school to engage in masculine social action and in turn he reproduced both structures through his masculine social action. Jerry was now accountably masculine, there was congruence between sex and gender, and the duality of structure and action transpired.

A Localized Positive Masculinity

I asked Jerry if he discussed this bullying and fighting with either parent, and he said "of course." In fact, all three—Mom, Dad, and Jerry—discussed the issue together after his first fight: "They sat me down and had a nice talk with me. They were like, 'Oh, we're really sorry,' and they told me it wasn't my fault when I was bullied and everything, and just to next time turn my back. Not to fight."

Q. Your parents didn't tell you to bully back or fight back?

A. No, my mom and dad never said that. My mom is against that, you know, the macho thing about guys that have to puff themselves all up and everything.

Q. Did your parents teach you to handle these kinds of problems in a nonviolent way?

A. Yeah. My mom wanted me to see that you didn't have to do that and my dad is the same way. We talked about it quite a bit. My parents would say, "It's the other kid's problem. There's something wrong with kids that bully kids."

At first Jerry reflexively decided not to accept his parents' suggestion and he chose to continue to respond in a physically violent way at school. Jerry explained that he internally determined he could not simply "walk away" because "you have to show kids you're not afraid to do it. My mom and dad didn't understand what it was like." Here we see Jerry reflexively negotiating a contradictory social situation: on the one hand he is confronted with the culturally significant masculine social structures among boys at school that emphasized "handling playground business" by fighting back and on the other hand he is challenged through a supplemental constraint and enabler in the form of intimate conversations with people he highly respects—his parents—who stressed turning his back to the bullies and walking away. The following extended dialogue demonstrates how reflexively Jerry eventually broke from the culturally influential social structures at school by accepting a nonviolent response to the masculine bullying challenges:

Q. After each fight did you talk to your parents about it?

A. Oh, yeah. We've always had a very open relationship.

Q. Both parents were telling you to just walk away, but at the same time you felt you could not because you had to show other kids that you were tough?

A. Right. My mom and dad said [to] walk away and the kids on the playground said show that you are tough. It was very confusing for a little kid.

Q. How did you resolve this dilemma?

A. My mom and dad had more and more of these talks with me, and around the fifth grade what they were saying began to sink in.

Q. It was the persistence of your parents then that changed your mind?

A. Yeah, and I did kind of experiments at school where if a kid started saying stuff I would just walk away. And that's when it really started to sink in. It was nice, and I'd come home and say to my parents, "Hey, you guys are right."

Q. When you walked away didn't the kids continue to bully and tease you?

A. Yeah, but I could deal with it because I knew that I wasn't going to get into trouble. Knowing that if they get caught telling me I'm a "wimp" and "fat ass" that they are going to be the ones in trouble. That felt good.

Q. But how did you deal with the idea that you may still be a wimp because you didn't fight back?

A. It was the talks with my parents. They'd reassure me that you were stronger to walk away than to put up your dukes and fight about it. And then I did that and I started to understand that "hey, they're right and it works."

Distancing himself from the influential relational and discursive social structures at school, Jerry draws on the intimate conversations with his parents—as a supplemental constraint and enabler—which eventually constrained Jerry from "fighting back" yet enabled him to resolve the contradiction by practicing an alternative response—to simply "walk away." Jerry determined through his conversations with his parents that "walking away" was actually a more compelling form of masculinity than was fighting back; indeed, unmanly behavior in the eyes of the dominant popular boys was now manly for Jerry.

Jerry indicated that his parents' emphasis on solving interpersonal problems in a nonviolent manner probably had something to do with the fact that his mother had subscribed to *Ms.* magazine and was "into the whole feminist thing." While attending part-time classes, Jerry's mother met a number of women and began to participate in a feminist support group. "There's like four or five women that she sees once or twice a month."

Q. Did your mother introduce you to some feminist ideas?

A. A couple of things 'cause she was taking women's studies classes.

Q. Did your mother teach you about how to handle the bullying?

A. Yeah. She'd be like, "Just brush it off." So that's how I kind of have gotten around it. It's just brushing it off. You know, I would say to myself, "there must be something wrong with this kid if they feel they have to make fun of me."

Q. So it was interaction with your mother that convinced you not to fight back when bullied?

A. Right. But Dad and Mom never encouraged fighting. I learned from them that if I was picked on I should find a different way to respond. Both Mom and Dad said that.

Despite the fact that Jerry continued to be the victim of bullying, these discussions with his parents convinced him to never again respond by fighting. Instead, he reflexively decided to simply walk away: "Usually it resolves itself. You just walk away and the kid doesn't even say anything to you because he can't get a rise out of you." Jerry reflexively concluded that this is the best way to handle such a situation. Although Jerry continued to be defined as subordinate in relation to the dominant masculine boys at school, he now felt confident responding this way because although the bullying continues "as you're walking away, later it's like you just don't even acknowledge that he's there." Jerry successfully opposed the in-school attempt by the dominant popular boys to subordinate him. Through his practice of "walking away" Jerry both challenged his position as "subordinate" in the "clique" masculine social structures and he refused to reproduce these social structures; instead, through reflexivity Jerry decided to break from both the relational and discursive social structures and practice an alternative nonviolent positive masculinity. Jerry reflexively distanced himself from these structures and was able to call both into question through a novel form of masculine social action.

Jerry first learned about sexuality when he was in seventh grade. "I was snooping around the house one day and I found that my parents had the *Joy of Sex* books, and so I looked at them a lot." He also heard from kids at school about heterosexuality: "Guys would talk about it all the time—having sex and stuff with girls." Jerry eventually decided to mention the books to his parents and several times they looked through them together. On one occasion Jerry and his parents were scanning through the books when they "came to these two girls that were having sex and I was like 'what's this?'" Jerry's parents explained that the women were lesbians and that "some people were into that kind of thing." When they told him that his sexual orientation was "up to him," he told his parents that he "always liked the female body." Because of the relational and discursive social structural emphasis on heterosexuality at school and at home, Jerry adopted what was in the offering and reflexively decided he is "straight." And he had two girlfriends in junior high school, one in seventh grade and one in eighth grade; neither friendship progressed beyond "going out on dates." He also learned through conversations with his parents that his two older cousins were gay and Jerry and his mother frequently would have tea with several gay and lesbian friends. In any event, there was arguably no "emphasis"—simply "balance"—and it is the combination of interaction at home in the form of a supplemental constraint and enabler and at school in the form of a culturally influential heterosexual relational and discursive social structure whereby Jerry reflexively decided to construct a positive heteromasculine project as his own that included an acceptance of same-sex sexuality.

Although successful in teaching Jerry how to handle interpersonal problems at school in a nonconflictual way, his parents continued to disagree over family finances. These disagreements escalated to the point where they decided that divorce was the only option. When Jerry was in the eighth grade his father moved out of the house. Jerry was extremely sad about the divorce but, as he put it, "there was still love and affection from both of them. It just wasn't at the same time." He continued to spend considerable time with both parents on a regular basis. "They'd always say, 'we're having our own problems and it's not your fault.'" Jerry never felt he was the cause of the divorce.

Jerry lived with his mother and visited his father on weekends until he was fifteen. Everything was fine in Jerry's life until he became what he describes as "lazy around the house." He refused to do most of the chores his mother asked him to do because "I had my own things I wanted to do. I wanted to hang out with my friends and go places, and she didn't want me to do that because she needed help at home and she was working"; consequently, his positive masculine project momentarily began to decline. During Jerry's eighth-grade year his mother was not home when he returned from school because of her work. Jerry was supposed to use this time for homework and chores. He would usually do his homework but only a few chores, and then he would play with his friends. Jerry liked his friends because "they accepted me for who I was."

Q. What did you like to do with your friends?

A. Ride snowmobiles and practice shooting guns. We had fun together 'cause we never teased or fought.

Q. But you didn't do your chores?

A. Right. I'd slack off. I wouldn't do the dishes, walk the dog. I'd just watch TV or hang out with my friends, because I didn't want to do my chores. I was irresponsible.

Q. And your mother would continue to ask you to help out with the household duties?

A. Yeah. She'd say, "It's important that you learn to do this now, because when you're older there isn't going to be anybody that wants to take care of you." And I was like, "Whatever. I'll find somebody." And then she just kept nagging me and getting mad at me because I was lazy. So I finally told her, "I want to move in with Dad."

Without the egalitarian relational and discursive social structures at home to draw from, then, Jerry reflexively decided to
"hang out" with his friends, he rejected doing most chores, and
eventually he moved in with his father during the early part of his
freshman year in high school. The bullying persisted in high
school but Jerry reflexively chose to never respond in a violent
way. The "walking away" reaction continued to work in the sense
that the verbal bullying did not disturb or trouble him in any way
and he felt comfortable engaging in this particular practice. The
most frequent verbal bullying Jerry experienced in high school
was being "called a fag a lot, and queer, and anything pertaining
to being homosexual. So I just shrug it off. I could yell at the kid
or something, but there's no point. He is just going to be narrow-
minded about it. So I just turn my back on it instead of putting up
the dukes." Accordingly, in high school Jerry was now constructed
as embodying a more specific and thoroughgoing femininity by
the dominant popular bullies because he did not "fight back," he
did not play sports, and he "hung out" with the "laid-back" crowd
(see below), yet he responded by personally orchestrating an alternative masculine response through the practice of walking
away—dualism rather than duality between structure and action
continued to be prevalent.

Nevertheless, because of the masculine nature of the relational
and discursive social structures, the in-school dominant bullies-
Jerry relationship constructed a culturally ascendant *dominating*
hegemonic masculinity and emphasized femininity relationship.
Like Sam, Jerry's feminized position in the "clique" relational and
discursive social structures is underpinned by his interactional
disconnect with the masculine structured action of fighting back
when bullied and participating in sports. Jerry chose not to engage in these masculine social practices in any way. Although
Jerry interprets his choice as an alternative and a formidably secure form of masculinity, to the in-school audience and the bul-

lies his behavior was coded as feminine. The dominant bullies embodied aggressiveness and a capacity to engage in violence while Jerry embodied passivity and the inability to engage in physical violence, both sets of gendered qualities situationally associated with masculinity and femininity respectively. Jerry was invested with situationally defined "inferior" gender qualities that assimilated with femininity and the bullies were invested with situationally defined "superior" qualities that assimilated with masculinity. Moeover, the bullies were commanding and controlling the interaction, they were exercising power and control over Jerry, they were "calling the shots" and "running the show." Consequently we have the cultural ascendancy of an in-school localized dominating hegemonic masculinity that circulates a legitimating discursive justification for gender inequality. And like Sam, Jerry is constructed as a hybridized "feminine boy."

In high school, then, Jerry continued to be bullied by the dominant "popular guys." As he put it, "The tough guys, the athletes, the macho guys." When I asked Jerry if he wanted to be like the "popular guys" he said, "At first I did. But then Mom and Dad told me, 'Just be your own person.' And that had a lot of influence on me. Plus I never really liked sports."

Q. You never liked sports?

A. Not really organized sports. I liked playing hockey, but not for a team.

Q. You just didn't want to participate in the organized aspect of sports?

A. You know in high school I see the locker room camaraderie. They walk around and snap each other's asses with towels and everything. I'm not really interested in that. And there is a lot of macho crap that goes on in the locker room and everything, and I just don't want to be part of that.

Q. Tell me about the other cliques in your high school.

A. The jocks are the popular guys because they get in the news for accomplishments they make in sports. It's like, "Hey, did you see so and so in the news the other day?" And then there are the brains which most people ignore. And then there are the loaders.

Q. What are loaders?

A. They are the mostly druggies. They're into pot and stuff. And then there are the homies or G-funks, because G is for gangsta. The G-funks think they're the tough guys.

Q. Which group are you in?

A. I'm not in a group. I have some friends that are loaders; we are kinda the laid-back crowd. But I'm not in any group 'cause it's like they all have something to prove. I've got nothing to prove. I am who I am, and if they don't like it—too bad.

Jerry also stated that there are numerous "feminine boys" in his school and, not surprisingly, "some" homophobia as well. Most people ignore these boys but occasionally they call them "fags."

Q. Are these boys gay?

A. I don't know if they are gay but they are kinda feminine. I get along with them real well but some guys constantly call them names like "fag" and "queer." I accept that some people are just like that and some of these feminine guys are in our laid-back group—I like them.

Q. But you consider yourself heterosexual?

A. Yeah. I just never had a sexual interest in guys. When I was younger I liked to play with my friends but I like never saw it in a sexual way. It wasn't until around seventh grade that I started to like girls. I became interested in their body then.

In high school Jerry was yet to have a date (he described himself as a "virgin") but had numerous girl *friends*. "There are a bunch of girls at school that I get along with. I treat them just like anybody else, just like my friends. We talk about what's going on in life and just hang out together."

Q. Do you ever hear kids at school talking about engaging in sex?

A. Oh, yeah. I hear that a lot. But it's like, "That's real tacky." If somebody is going to brag about that then I'm sorry to hear it. There is more to life than getting a piece of ass.

Q. So sexuality isn't something that is important to you?

A. I think sex is pretty much important to everybody. It's part of life, but not right now. I'm more interested in bringing my grades up in school than having sex.

Q. What are your plans after high school?

A. I'm going to have a family. I'm going to enjoy raising my kids. There are just so many things out there that I want to do that seem like fun. I'd love to race motorcycles. I'd love to have a dogsled team. There are just so many things out there that I'd love to do. I'm gonna start a business like Dad's, and then who knows where I could go!

Jerry continued to be labelled feminine by the dominant boys because of his particular type of masculine construction in school. However, his interaction with the laid-back group and his other friends proved to be accepting of his sex appearance and gender practices—indeed, incongruence between sex and gender was embraced by this group—and thus Jerry's positive masculinity and hybridization were thoroughly welcomed and supported. The "laid-back crowd" included both boys and girls who refrained from any bullying about the shape and size of bodies and all members of this group never engaged in violent behavior. This laid-back group accepted sexual diversity—including Jerry's celibacy—and they were not misogynist, homophobic, nor hierarchical, and there was no emphasis in this group on constructing hegemonic, dominant, or dominating masculinities. The laid-back group seemed to celebrate their difference from, rather than their inferiority to, the dominant boys and girls in the school. In other words, this laid-back group constructed equality gender relations at school and Jerry actualized these relations by engaging in similar forms of social action which collectively composed his positive masculinity. And once again the duality of structure and action materialized.

Let us now turn to chapter 4 where I present the life histories of two individuals who identify as genderqueer.

4

GENDERQUEERS: JESSIE AND MORGAN

This chapter investigates two white young adults from New England—Jessie and Morgan (both pseudonyms)—who self-identify as *genderqueer,* meaning they consider oneself as *both* masculine and feminine (Jessie) or as *neither* masculine nor feminine (Morgan). I begin with Jessie.

JESSIE

Jessie is twenty-one years old, a fourth year undergraduate university student, is tall and average weight, has short sandy hair, and came to both interviews in androgynous attire. Jessie identifies as genderqueer and defines genderqueer as "someone who is read and addressed as either male or female, masculine or feminine, or masculine and feminine, depending upon the context."

A Localized Positive Tomboy Masculinity

Jessie grew up in a middle-class home; both her parents worked in professional positions. Jessie spent considerable time with her parents but in particular helped her father with "the masculine

stuff around the house—like build[ing] a playhouse in the back-
yard and one Christmas my dad got me a tool bench and some
tools!" Jessie was also very close to her mother because "she set
the boundaries for me of how to be female in the world."

In her early childhood Jessie understood herself as female but
her mother also taught her that she did not have to be "extremely
feminine." Jessie expanded on this topic: "I saw in my mother that
she wasn't feminine in the way that society says. The way she
handled herself emotionally and her attitude to the world and her
personality characteristics all are generally associated with masculinity. She was very confident, courageous, and assertive, and all
this has an undertone of masculinity in our culture. And she
passed that down to me." Jessie never felt pressure to be "completely feminine because my mother didn't succumb to it." Jessie
reflexively drew on the relational and discursive social structures
prevalent at home that emphasized the binary conception of sex
and thus she came to understand herself as "a girl," yet she simultaneously concluded that it would devalue her agency if she engaged in femininity and thus Jessie resolved that it is only acceptable for "a girl to be masculine." Jessie went on to point out that
"sometimes I would wear makeup and dresses," but "mostly I
enjoyed wearing sporty clothes, playing sports, and just do[ing]
what boys do, and my parents supported it. I was taught that I
could do anything I want to do."

Jessie relished this early childhood notion of hybridized gender—wearing feminine or sporty clothing yet practicing a localized in-home tomboy masculinity—and she noticed at a very
young age "that I would be supported by both my parents and
family friends, who never criticized me for looking like a girl and
not acting feminine. So I felt supported by the way my mother set
an example and through the lack of criticism I got from other
adults." In fact, Jessie reflexively concluded that looking feminine
and acting masculine was normal behavior: "My parents taught

me that I was a girl but it was okay for me to act masculine; it was normal to me because my mother was that way." And consequently Jessie reflexively actualized through practice these in-home social structures—Jessie labeled her social action "tomboy masculinity" (although her family never used the word tomboy). When I asked her why, she replied: "My parents' attitude toward gender was men and women can both do masculine things. My mom did all kinds of masculine things, yet my mom wore makeup and dresses, so I kinda imitated her. So there definitely was room in my house for us women to do masculine things, and that felt good. I didn't have one way of being shoved down my throat; I could have been feminine probably, but my mom and I were 'tomboys' at home and we both enjoyed doing masculine things." Incongruence between sex and gender was acceptable and thus normal in Jessie's in-home setting.

Jessie grew up in a family environment that emphasized egalitarian gender relations. Both parents worked outside the home in professional positions and both equally participated in domestic labor. Jessie observed and reflexively appropriated from this combined relational and discursive social structure the celebration of in-home masculine practices and the notion that both males and females can and should if they desired engage in masculine practices—through her social action Jessie reproduced that structure and thus the duality of structure and action was prevalent.

As early as age four Jessie reflexively deduced that there are only two types of people in the world: male and female. In addition to the social structure discussed above, a further occasion for this determination was the birth of her younger brother. One of the first questions she asked her parents was: "Why does he have that thing between his legs [penis] and I don't?" And they responded that he has a penis because he is a boy and she does not have one because she is a girl. So Jessie adopted from this conversation a binary conception of sex that the *only* two types of people in the world are distinguished by the existence of a penis—a person with a penis is male, and a person without a penis is female—and therefore as Jessie put it: "I'm a girl."

Jessie enjoyed a very happy, secure, and attached family life in which she felt comfortable discussing many different issues with both parents. "They were wonderfully supportive and loving parents!" And when I asked Jessie about power relations at home, she answered: "No one person really had more power than any other. My parents made about the same amount of money and they also always decided things together. They always discussed before making decisions and would even ask me for my opinion when I was older. And of course when I was younger they had power over me, but not really since I was a teenager. I could do what I wanted, and I never got in trouble—I was a good kid."

It was in the home setting then that Jessie's family embodied gender equality and Jessie reflexively adopted what was structurally offered. Jessie first began to practice at home a hybridized positive "tomboy masculine" project as her own. She did this by engaging in self-control over her life yet imitating her mother and thus embodying this type of positive gender construction through her perceived female sex appearance and her masculine gender practices.

At school Jessie encountered a somewhat unsettling social situation as the binary conception of sex Jessie learned at home "really took off in second grade" because it was here that Jessie remembered "kids first saying to me, 'You really do x, y, and z,' meaning boy stuff, 'well for being a girl, but you should really do a, b, and c well,' meaning girl stuff." At home Jessie determined that she is a girl who was also good at doing what was considered to be "boy stuff," yet throughout elementary and junior high school Jessie continually was "reminded" by classmates that because she performed in-school masculine practices well and for the most part rejected feminine practices and fashion, she was therefore "different" from most other girls. At school there emerged a tension between her sex category and gender behavior and Jessie eventually came to associate that difference with, and identify as, a tomboy. I asked Jessie why she decided to identify this way:

> It was a label kids at school gave me, and I thought it through and decided that it seemed to make sense because it corresponded with the privileging of masculinity in my house; even if you are female-bodied, it's okay to have masculine personality traits and do what boys do, and so they celebrated that by encouraging it in me over and over again, which in turn empowered me to emphasize being masculine. So I did what was comfortable for me at home and school, I did what I wanted to do which were things that garnered people at school to think of me—and for me to think of myself—as a tomboy. At home I wasn't seen as different but at school I was.

Although Jessie accepts an essentialist notion of the "female body," she is revealing for us the institutionalization of gender relations in her school whereby she is positioned as subordinate—without her own volition and effort—within the "clique" relational and discursive social structures of the school. Reflexively negotiating her positioning in these structures Jessie decides to continue to engage in tomboy hybridized gendered practices because in part such practices corresponded to home interaction, because of her sense of self-determination and individuality, and because she simply enjoyed doing so. Nevertheless, this tomboy identity at school often and early on resulted in Jessie being bullied first by the dominant popular boys: "Yeah, I mean the boys at school started to bully me because they didn't like that I was good at sports, but I didn't let them push me around. So they would say all the time 'I should just act like a girl' and 'stop trying to be a boy,' and they'd say other horrible things to me, like 'do you have a penis?' I was never invited to parties and stuff or to be part of the popular groups."

Eventually the dominant popular girls likewise began to bully Jessie as well for her "difference." When I specifically asked Jessie how she was different from the popular girls she stated that she often wore sports clothes to school, such as sweatpants, sweatshirts, and tennis shoes, no makeup, and she had very short hair. Although both Jessie and the popular dominant girls often played on the same sports teams and her popular teammates were also, like Jessie, "full of confidence, knew what they wanted and how to get it," the popular dominant girls "all had long hair, wore makeup, and always wore girlie type of clothes." Jessie therefore stood out as "different" and certain dominant boys and now dominant girls at school would verbally bully her: "'You look gross because you look like a guy,' is what they would say, stuff like that." This subordination—and thus a publicly identified unacceptable incongruence between sex and gender according to the bullies— continued throughout elementary and into junior high school. I asked Jessie how this made her feel and she replied: "I didn't really like the popular [dominant] girls anyway because they were too feminine acting, they always wore stupid sexy clothes, and they always just talked about boys and the way they looked. So I just hung out with a few girls like me, other tomboys, and we had fun together."

Jessie here is distancing herself from the feminine aspects of the "clique" in-school relational and discursive social structures. She is breaking from these culturally ascendant structures and in the process resisting them. Dualism rather than duality takes place and Jessie in turn reflexively decides to join together with other like-minded girls. Jessie and her tomboy friends never bullied each other, they were very accepting of all members of the group, they accepted their hybrid masculine constructions, and "we all liked doing the same things, like wearing boys' clothes and short hair and playing boys and girls sports."

Jessie identified five major "cliques" in her elementary and junior high school: "The 'rich kids' and 'jocks' were the most popular kids, the 'smart kids,' the 'goths,' and 'druggies,' and a whole bunch of kids who were seen as 'weird' in some way. Me and my tomboy girlfriends were in this last group." Finding herself subordinated as "weird" within the informal yet culturally significant "clique" social structures at school—the subordination resulting from Jessie challenging those structures by embodying tomboyism—Jessie reflexively negotiated in particular the femininity constructed by the dominant popular girl-bullies and reflexively chose instead to continue practicing tomboyism and to "hang out" with other tomboy girls. This also meant wearing boys' clothes and rejecting much of dominant femininity by practicing "boy stuff," such as playing both boys and girls sports. Jessie was similar to the dominant girls through her independence, confidence, and assertiveness yet she was different in her gender display and practices. Jessie was unaccountably feminine and therefore subordinated early on at school, yet she reflexively decided not to give in to the bullies and thus chose instead to participate in the tomboy group. And it was here whereby Jessie was accountable, because incongruence between sex and gender is acceptable in this group and the tomboys seemed to celebrate their difference from, while denying their subordination to, the dominant girls.

Yet despite her ongoing friendship with other tomboy girls, the bullying continued. Jessie therefore decided to seek advice from her parents. Both counseled her to "ignore the bullies, hang out with people who respect me like my 'tomboy' friends, and they said it was actually beneficial for me to do what I enjoyed, to be myself, to be my own person, so I did." Jessie continued on this topic:

> I took seriously what my parents said and decided not to let it bother me at all because my parents reinforced that the bullies were just jealous and bullying was a way for them to deal with their own insecurities. And so I just thought that these kids see qualities in me that they would like to see in themselves. So that actually meant to me that my masculine qualities are good and the femininity of the popular girls is bad. I didn't like their girlie stuff and the things they did, so I decided to follow my parents' advice and just ignore people when they said stuff and just hang out with my tomboy friends.

Jessie reflexively drew on the supplemental constraint and enabler of intimate conversations with individuals she highly respected—her parents. These conversations supported Jessie's decision to ignore the bullies but simultaneously enabled her to "hang out" with her tomboy friends. Jessie therefore refused to accept and participate in the in-school social structures—she distanced herself from these structures and reflexively chose instead to interact exclusively with her tomboy friends.

Around age twelve Jessie noticed that her breasts were now changing somewhat yet she felt insecure about their size: "My breasts weren't big enough. I would look at other girls who were more developed and then that would make me feel really self-conscious and that I'm really flat-chested, and so I felt different in a new way now." Although Jessie continued to identify as a tomboy, she began to have more serious inner dialogues about whether or not she was a "real girl" because of what she perceived as a lack of developing breasts.

Q. Did puberty impact you at all?

A. Yeah, it really did. It changed things because I started to compare myself to other girls and I didn't match up with things like my breast size, and it made me feel more like I wasn't one of them. And I was real late in having periods, like four years after my friends did. I could still do the things I always wanted to do, like play baseball and rollerblade, and I could still be the independent, strong, and confident tomboy I always was and I wanted to be. But I did think a lot about being a girl and not looking like a girl, and that started to bother me more and more. Like why don't I have breasts like other girls, why don't I have periods, and why do I like masculine stuff? I started to really think about that.

For Jessie, her body at this time in her life now became a supplemental constraint and enabler on her practice by creating a contradiction—she pictured herself as a girl yet she did not recognize herself as embodying femaleness because of her comparisons with other girls at school. After internally mulling over this ongoing contradictory dilemma, Jessie reflexively decided "that since I don't have a penis then I must be a girl. So I thought I'm a girl, just a different type of girl who doesn't have breasts. But I was still kinda confused." Jessie's changing body—or lack there of—became incompatible with her fundamental sense of self—"I'm a girl"—and she resolved this contradiction by reflexively deciding that since she does not possess a penis then she must instead be a "girl," but a girl "who doesn't have breasts."

Through interaction at school Jessie also observed classmates engaging in heterosexual boyfriend/girlfriend relations and heard their "sex talk" about "hugging, kissing, and sex and stuff" and the idea that "if you were really close to a boy and emotionally intimate with a boy and you are a girl, then you are supposed to be boyfriend and girlfriend. And since all my friends were dating boys then I'm supposed to date boys." It was this interaction with the culturally ascendant heterosexual relational and discursive social structures at school that was Jessie's initial knowledge about sexuality and thus her sexual awakening. Jessie adopted what was offered by this structure and in turn attempted to affix a heterosexual project to her tomboy masculine project through practice:

"I decided to attend school dances because since I'm a girl I should find a boyfriend like all the other girls." Jessie is reflexively drawing on the in-school culturally significant heterosexual boy-friend-girlfriend social structure and in combination with her internal self-attribution as a "girl" Jessie decided she now wants to be a participant in such heterosexual relations.

Eventually Jessie did meet a number of boys who she dated, yet the interaction was always the same: "We would go to dances together and kiss and go on other dates, but then after a short time we'd break up because they'd always say, 'Why can't you be like other girls? And how come you look different and act different from other girls?'" Jessie interpreted such comments as meaning, "Why can't you be more sexy in the way you look and act?" And Jessie always responded: "'I like being me and this is me.' Kinda like, 'What you see is what you get.'" All the boys Jessie dated were aggressive and dominating and as she reported: "They just decided everything. When we went out they decided where we would go and what we would do. And they decided when we would kiss and have sex and stuff. They controlled everything and did it all their way. They always said that's the way it should be, and I didn't want anyone controlling anything about me. They didn't allow me any space to express and assert my desires and needs. So in the end and after thinking this through, I would just break up with these guys." Jessie wanted to equally decide what they would and would not do together, and she also wanted to be assertive sexually but these boys disallowed such agency. So following reflexive deliberations Jessie broke from and resisted participation in the heterosexual boyfriend/girlfriend re-lational and discursive social structures and put a stop to all of these heterosexual relationships. Consequently, dualism between structure and action transpired in the process and Jessie contin-ued to construct her particular hybrid form of gender.

This experience with boys striving to dominate relationships and pressure Jessie into practicing subordination—and thereby attempting to construct gender hegemonic relations—eventually resulted in her refusal altogether to date boys (she seemingly concluded that *all* heterosexual relations will be oppressive), and she continued to act and dress in any way "that did not look feminine at all, because I just hated girlie clothes and I just lost interest in guys being attracted to me because what's the point, you know?" In essence, then, Jessie chose to continue constructing what was labeled in this setting as incongruence between her sex and gender.

A Localized Protective Hegemonic Masculinity

By age fifteen when Jessie entered high school, she continued to see herself as a girl, "but a different type of girl because I didn't like being with guys and I didn't want to be feminine like most other girls, so I really saw myself as different." Jessie indicated that in high school something new occurred: she often heard derogatory comments about same-sex relationships, "like people being called 'fags' and 'lesbos' and how gay people don't like to be with the opposite sex and how gays are like girls and lesbians are like guys, you know, stuff like that." Jessie went on to point out that "this all started to hit home with me because I felt different from other girls, you know, having small breasts, not having a period until I was 16, liking to do guy stuff, and didn't like being with guys, but also I didn't have a penis. So I was confused to say the least. And then I started to think that hey, maybe I'm a lesbian." Jessie internally deliberated about this "over and over again" and eventually she decided to talk with her mother who responded in the following way: "She said maybe I was a lesbian and what's the big deal, and that I should feel free to explore all sexual options. That if I don't like boys, then that's okay. And she was real understanding about it and said I should just act on my desires, so I did."

This conversational supplemental constraint and enabler had a major impact on Jessie because at this time she was on the girls' soccer team throughout high school and shortly after the above conversation with her mother Jessie and a teammate developed a very close, friendly relationship. Eventually Jessie became attracted to this teammate "because she was fun to be with." Every day after soccer practice Jessie and her new friend would walk home together, and then one day during their walk home the following interaction took place:

> I started to think that I would really like to kiss and hug her body but I knew I couldn't. And then she told me she didn't really like dating guys, and then I said, "I don't either!" And then we just embraced and really hugged each other and we kissed. We then started dating, and both of us came out together as lesbians.

> Q. How did you decide to come out as lesbians?

> A. Well, we talked about it, and neither of us liked dating guys and we both felt different from other girls and we were really attracted to each other, and we talked about what kids were saying, so we decided we must be lesbians because that's what people called two girls attracted to each other. And we really liked each other and we didn't care what other people thought, so we decided together to tell the world!

Jessie and her friend drew on the culturally ascendant heterosexual-homosexual relational and discursive social structures—they seemingly were unaware of other possible sexual identities—at school to appropriate a lesbian identity and relationship and in turn they reproduced these structures through their social action—duality now materialized between structure and action. Following this identity becoming public, Jessie found that some students at school—while accepting of the relationship—nevertheless asked, "Well, who's the man in the relationship?" Jessie told me she understood this question as "Who is the assertive and confident one in the relationship?" And Jessie's answer was, "I'm that person." Jessie then elaborated on this: "I was, vis-à-vis my girlfriend, the assertive and confident one and she was the passive and shy one. My girlfriend looked up to me as her 'knight in shining armor' who watched over her. I wasn't domineering at all, just more self-assured than her; kinda 'caring self-confidence' is how I describe it—I was her support. So I liked this relationship because I could be the masculine one; that's what I eventually figured out. And I looked and acted masculine and she looked and acted feminine. So we were a normal couple with female bodies."

Q. Did other students recognize you as a "normal" couple?

A. Oh yeah, everyone was accepting of it and they saw me as the masculine one and she as the feminine one. Everyone was cool about it.

In this relationship, then, Jessie derives her masculine power through the dependent status of her girlfriend; Jessie's girlfriend respects, honors, and yields to the caring guidance and support Jessie offers and indeed embraces her hybrid gender construction. Here feminine subordination and gender hegemony proceeds from Jessie's position as compassionate protector and the relationship centers on clearly defined and enacted masculine and feminine practices—and this binary reproduced by Jessie and her friend is additionally accepted by her classmates.

This construction of gender hegemony was also manifested in their sexual relationship. Jessie and her girlfriend had sex many times but "it was me doing sexual things to her, I was the top and she was the bottom, I was the sexually aggressive one and she was the passive one, I always initiated sex and she followed." Jesse explained that they both would be sexually satisfied, yet it was the particular sexual practices of Jessie that accomplished this sexual contentment. Jessie volunteered some examples: "Like, I always did the fucking, you know, rubbing my genitals against hers and then we'd both get off. And I'd always go down on her, not her on me." Although these sexual practices are not inherently gendered or hierarchical, Jessie and her girlfriend construct them as such, which is made more explicit in the following dialogue:

Q. Was gender related to this?

A. Yeah, it was. I was the guy and she was the girl and I figured out that I became attracted to her because she was very feminine and I saw myself as masculine. I figured out that I was attracted to her in terms of someone wanting to be taken care of, someone who needed a partner who is strong and takes charge, but again in a very caring and supportive way. And I wanted to be that strong person and I really enjoyed taking charge. And this confirmed how much being masculine meant to me.

Q. Did you consider yourself butch?

A. Not at all because I didn't even know that term then. I just really liked taking care of her in so many ways and kinda being her protector. And I liked being the masculine one, even when we have sex.

This sexual interaction between Jessie and her girlfriend then is *complicit* with her localized *protector* hegemonic masculinity but because of its privatized nature it does not construct hegemony. In both her private sexual and public nonsexual interaction with her girlfriend, Jessie was the benevolently assertive leader and confident protective partner while her girlfriend was the timid and passive protected follower. Jessie constructed publicly—in relation to her girlfriend—localized situationally defined "superior" qualities that assimilated with masculinity and her girlfriend constructed publicly—in relation to Jessie—localized situationally defined "inferior" qualities that assimilated with femininity. Jessie moved then from a subordinate tomboy masculine position to a protective hegemonic masculine place within the public setting of the school. The public relationship—but not the private relationship—contributed to the circulation of a legitimating justification for gender inequality.

Jessie and her girlfriend stayed together as a homonormative couple throughout high school—"we went to the prom together"—and both had numerous straight friends and the dominant popular group accepted both. The embodied incongruence between sex and gender was accepted primarily because of their binary masculine-feminine relationship. Nevertheless, Jessie and her girlfriend mutually broke off their partnership at the end of the summer following high school graduation "because we went our separate ways to different universities." By the end of this relationship, however, Jessie "realized how much masculinity meant to me. I wanted to be and do everything masculine because this was me. I figured out that ever since I was a kid I loved to do masculine stuff and now that really took off." In other words, reflexively Jessie is identifying here a major transition occurring in her life whereby masculinity now supersedes sex as her fundamental project; masculinity replaced sex ("I'm a girl") as her primary internal self-attribution while sex now becomes secondary. And Jessie attached same-sex sexuality to her notion of masculinity as now a fixed and permanent part of her identity.

Both Masculine *and* Feminine

During Jessie's first semester at university she enrolled in an Introduction to Women and Gender Studies course and "loved it." I asked Jessie what she liked about the course and she responded: "I didn't know anything about gender and sexual oppression and never thought about things that way. In high school my girlfriend and I were finally accepted by most people. But I never saw it as sexual oppression, I just saw it as us being normal yet different, you know. But then I started understanding about systemic sexism, racism, classism, and homophobia. And this was my first springboard into social justice, you know: 'I'm gay; I'm oppressed.'"

In this course Jessie established some new friendships and as she put it: "All of sudden I had like these five major friends who identified as transmen or genderqueer and who were also polyamorous, and all of us would hang out a lot and talk about trans and queer issues." Jessie's new friends emphasized gender and sexual diversity rather than dichotomy, and Jessie reflexively embraced and actualized these relations through her social action. Jessie recounted that "although I was a political science major I fit in wonderfully with these folks because I was a masculine lesbian and we would have these awesome conversations about ambiguity and feeling in the middle of things, and not fitting into one or the other category completely." All of Jessie's new friends "identified as transmasculine folks at various stages of transition," and Jessie engaged in numerous conversations with them about "what they thought of their bodies and how it related to other people." Through this interaction Jessie reflexively began to "question identities and binary thinking, and I was being supported by my new friends and so I thought I should study myself like everyone else. So I started really thinking about my identity, you know, like am I butch, trans, or what, and how does all this relate to my love of being masculine?" These conversations—as supplemental constraints and enablers—coalesced in enabling Jessie to think more seriously about and begin to question her current gender and sexual identities.

Jessie first internally explored "how I really feel and what my gender identity really means and what sexuality is and isn't." Jessie stated that the numerous verbal communications with her new transmasculine friends "led me to think at first about transitioning because I thought about my masculine presentation and stuff like hormones and breast surgery and coming out later. And so after a lot of conversations with my transmasculine friends and with myself I decided to start binding and wearing more elaborate male clothes and go out and try to pass as male. I was experimenting to see if I liked it." Jessie learned about binding, breast surgery, and hormones from the conversations with her transmasculine friends, so she decided to attempt "passing as male to see if I wanted to transition." Because for Jessie masculinity is now seemingly fixed and solid she begins to experiment aligning her body (sex) with her masculine (gender) identity to see if she actually should transition to male. I asked Jessie how attempting to "pass" as male affected her:

> Well I finally figured out after all these conversations and the experimenting that I really wanted to be gender fluid. I liked being masculine and looking male, but I also wanted people to question their own understanding of what I am, what my body represents, and you can't just assume I am some particular sex or gender. I connected back to when I was a tomboy and now a lesbian and how I enjoyed being masculine with girlfriends. But I also thought about that I'm female-bodied but also I've never been a traditional girlie girl, I've always been kinda both—I'm assertive but also very emotional—so I started to see myself in the middle, you know, a combination of masculine and feminine.

Jessie said interaction and conversations with her five trans-masculine friends was "a revelation" because they helped her understand the meaning of being a tomboy, why she did not like to be with boys, and why she liked sex with feminine women—"because I liked being masculine. And with my transmasculine friends I could really express the masculine part of me, but at the same time I'm female-bodied and I always liked my female body even if it was confusing at times. So, for the first time I found the *real me,* and people were accepting of the *real me,* which is a female-bodied person who likes masculinity." Not surprisingly, Jessie decided *not* to transition.

Q. Did your transmasculine friends try to push you in one direction?

A. Not at all. They just were very supportive that I could be whatever I want to be. Around my transmasculine friends I felt freedom to describe how I felt and I didn't feel obligated to become any one thing.

Q. So you weren't pressured to fit a particular narrative?

A. Not at all. We actually talked about "the script" or "the trans narrative" and I learned that I could create my own narrative, there was no right or wrong way, it was up to me. So I decided I'm in between. I decided that genderqueer was the best way to describe my identity. Genderqueer was very comfortable. Starting as a female-bodied person in this world and then coming into a sense of masculinity—I think genderqueer works for this. And I can be masculine when I want and feminine when I want—it's perfect!"

Eventually Jessie and her transmasculine friends—two of whom also identified as genderqueer—would regularly go out at night in drag: "It's what we like to do sometimes. And sometimes

I'd be totally masculine like put facial hair on, binding and packing, and go out to clubs and parties or just out in it, you know.
And then sometimes I'd go out very feminine, lotsa makeup, a
long wig, tight top and short skirt, stockings and high heels. But
most of the time when we go out I'm androgynous—I put on the
wig and facial hair but no binding or packing, but a tight top,
short skirt, and tennis shoes or other combinations. We are genderqueers because we queer gender, we disrupt the normal. It's
all about making people question me and themselves. We are
gender outlaws, we make people aware that gender is fluid."
Through the conversations and interactions with the five transmasculine friends, Jessie became an accountable and thus practicing transmasculine genderqueer—a specific form of hybrid gender construction. Jessie enjoys not "passing" as a male but rather
takes pleasure in fashioning herself as a gender hybrid. Jessie
approaches masculinity through signifiers and practices but never
completely "passes" as a man. And that is Jessie's goal, to approxi-
mate yet destabilize and unsettle any intelligible construction of
masculinity. I specifically asked Jessie if she learned about transgender and/or queer theory at school and she replied: "Not at all.
I was a poli-sci major and only took one women's studies course
and we just learned about race, gender, and sexual oppression. I
learned about genderqueer from my friends."

Jessie's definition of genderqueer is "one who is read and addressed as either male or female, masculine or feminine, or masculine *and* feminine, depending upon the context" and, therefore,
Jessie changes sex and gender according to the particular situation. I asked Jessie for additional examples and she mentioned
that when she goes to work she wears makeup and fashionable
feminine clothing and she is recognized as female, "but a very
confident and assertive female." In the context of work, then, "I
present as feminine, but I'm very self-assured and strong-willed.
I'm easily identified as female, and I'm dressed in a fashionably

feminine way, but I act like men do. So I combine masculinity and femininity. This way, people at work see me for who I am, that I'm not just one gender but both. That's me."

Consequently, through interaction with her five transmasculine friends, Jessie now no longer considers masculinity as exclusively her fundamental project. Rather, fluidity is now foundational, but in a binary way: "Sometimes I'm masculine, sometimes feminine, but most of the time both." Masculinity therefore remains a component of her genderqueer identity but it is now only a partial aspect of that identity. And such incongruence between sex and gender is acceptable within the context of Jessie's transmasculine friends.

Jessie and her current partner live together and "at home our relationship overall is equal as we are both sensitive to each other's needs, feelings, and wants; we both sacrifice for each other; and we both share the financial burden, the household chores, and the emotional and physical care for each other. And there's no gender dichotomy—we're both masculine and feminine. It's a relationship that's equal."

In addition to this egalitarian relational social structure at home that they both reproduce, Jessie and her partner also practice polyamory, which means "she's my primary partner but we don't believe in marriage and we see other people, but when we are together, we're very egalitarian in terms of giving and receiving." As Jessie further put it:

> We're very balanced regarding sexuality. We're 50/50 regarding top position. Sometimes I'll wear a strap on and sometimes she will. We both give and receive, we both penetrate and receive, and we both equally initiate sex. We play with gender during sex. Sometimes I give her "blow jobs" and sometimes she does it to me. And I "go down on her" and she does the same to me. We take on masculine and feminine roles depending on how we feel.

Beyond this egalitarian sexual relationship, Jessie reported that she adopted polyamory because it does not lock her into any particular form of sexuality: "I think sex is sex and it's not about a sexual orientation. The things you do during sex can definitely be about particular orientations, such as the actual sexual acts you engage in, but the idea and concept of 'having sex' with someone is not."

Jessie told me that recently she engaged in sexuality with "a few male-bodied people" and the sexuality was never "simply penile/vaginal missionary position intercourse. I've done a lot of different things with guys." Jessie offered an example:

During sex with these guys I sometimes present as masculine and sometimes I don't. And when I'm masculine I deliberately ask for male pronouns and so these guys would masculinize me when having sex with me. We engaged in penetration, but then it was always me on top, I was fucking them. You see, sexuality for me is not necessarily about our bodies, our sex, or our orientation because I like a lot of different sex acts with a lot of different people.

Q. Does having breasts and not having a penis impact your masculinity at all during sexuality?

A. Not at all because it's not all about being masculine. I can be masculine without having a penis; masculinity is fluid even during sex. Like I just said, even if a guy penetrates me, I'm controlling the penetration, not him. I'm on top and deciding how that penis is being used—I *gender*queer it, I *gender*queer sex. And so I can be masculine but also have a vagina and breasts. That's the whole point, I'm both, not one or the other. Plus, I'm not interested in being male, and the breasts and vagina are there and they are very much a part of my sexuality.

Q. Can you give me another example?

A. Yeah, sure. One male-bodied person I had sex with uses male pronouns but identifies as femme, and so I'm really attracted to gender ambiguity and queer people in general. And with him I presented as femme, asked for feminine pronouns, but I also fucked him and he fucked me. So I'm most comfortable sexually with people who allow a lot of fluidity in a lot of things and are really comfortable with themselves and comfortable with people who want to be whatever way they want to be. So we were fluid in our fucking and at the same time we both enjoyed my breasts together and we both enjoyed his cock. So it's always very fluid and it's always a combination of masculinity and femininity.

Q. What does masculinity mean to you now?

A. Since I'm genderqueer I'm both masculine and feminine and so masculinity is now only *one* piece of my gender, it's no longer *the* piece. So my masculinity is always associated with my femininity, they always go together: My masculinity is always a tender masculinity that's aggressive but not dominating and overpowering; it's confident but also very respectful, caring, and tender toward others in terms of the way I am; it's other-oriented, meaning I think of other people—I think of how my actions and words may affect other people, so I'm very respectful. But I also value myself in my words and actions in a way that is masculine, such as taking up space and presence in the world. I don't define this in terms of entitlement, but I feel I have a right to be here and when I'm doing something I have the right to do it. I'm very assertive but I'm also very emotional. But because I'm sensitive to my partner's needs and wants, my masculinity consists of a combination of confidence and caring and entails negotiation not dominance. It always goes together with my femininity.

MORGAN

Morgan is twenty-five years old, an undergraduate university student, petite with short curly dark hair, and like Jessie, she came to both interviews in androgynous attire. Morgan identifies as genderqueer and she defined genderqueer as "being gender fluid so that I express many genders in a multifaceted way."

A Localized Positive Tomboy Masculinity

Morgan grew up in a working-class family and both parents worked outside the home: her father was a factory worker and her mother was a receptionist. Morgan was very close to both parents, and the whole family—she has a younger brother by two years—often did "family things" together, such as camping and hiking, going to movies, playing games both indoors and outdoors, and sharing in domestic chores. There was little emphasis on gender difference in her household and therefore like Jessie, Morgan never felt pressured "to act like a girl at home." For example, when the family went camping "me and my mother always put the tents up and started the fire in the fire pit and my brother and father set up the camp kitchen and actually did most of the cooking." Morgan's chores at home ranged from helping both parents cook and clean up after each meal to taking out the garbage, shoveling snow in the winter, and mowing the lawn in the summer. By engaging in these chores Morgan reflexively draws on the egalitarian relational and discursive social structures at home to construct social action and in turn it is through these particular social actions that the social structures are reproduced.

Morgan described her childhood family life as "nonviolent, easygoing, and supportive" and as a "gender-neutral time period" in which she did not dress in feminine clothing but rather exclusively "dressed like the boys. My friends were both boys and girls, but not the popular kids, and we all did boy things together." Nevertheless, through interaction as a young child, Morgan learned that some people are male and some female and that the distinction between the two is based on bodily differences. As Morgan recalled: "At around age five or six I had a friend who was a boy and we would compare our bodies, and we discovered our difference—he had a penis and I didn't—and I never really thought about that difference before. So it became 'show me yours and I'll show you mine.' We would do it now and then in the basement of my house, and that's how I learned I was a girl." From this interaction Morgan felt enabled to conclude that there are two types of people in the world: those who have a penis (male) and those who do not (female).

By age ten Morgan was being labeled a tomboy by her classmates at school and her parents were always supportive of this gender label, as was Morgan. And Morgan described her hybrid tomboy practices as involving "just only interested in boys' clothes, never wore dresses, and doing only boy things, like riding bikes with friends, and we'd be gone like all day, playing catch and sports, and even wrestling with guys. I didn't have any interest in girl clothes and what girls do."

Morgan also mentioned that she always wore a baseball cap to school and finally was told by a teacher that she could not wear it inside the school building. Morgan and her father went to see the principal the next day, and "both of us wore baseball caps during our meeting with him. And my father was so cool—he convinced the principal to allow me to wear my cap in school." Morgan and her father were very close and often went fishing together, he taught her how to ride a bike, they frequently played catch, and they built a tree house together. So both of Morgan's parents supported her tomboy display and practice. When I asked Morgan if she enjoyed being a tomboy, she responded: "I did. I knew there was a difference between me and boys, but I never saw it as limiting what I could do. Because my parents were so supportive, I felt I could do anything I wanted and I really loved to do what people called 'boys' stuff,' and it was just more comfortable to wear boys' clothes. So I just saw the label as indicating who I am."

Like Jessie's parents (and Jerry's in chapter 3), then, Morgan's family embodied a relational and discursive social structure emphasizing gender equality and Morgan adopted—for the most part reflexively—what was structurally offered and in turn reproduced that social structure through her social action—duality between structure and action materialized yet she reflexively purposely practiced incongruence between sex and gender. It was in this egalitarian setting that Morgan first began to practice a positive hybrid tomboy gender project through her perceived female sex appearance and her masculine gender display and practices. Morgan told me that at home she could "choose how to be and to go after it, to be laid back but also stubborn in not letting others push me around, and to be confident in myself." Yet Morgan's tomboyism at home was different from Jessie's in the sense that Morgan did not construct femininity at all but, rather, she eschewed femininity altogether and fashioned an exclusive masculinity, although she and others recognized her as "a girl." Thus, like Jessie, initially Morgan adopted a sex identity as "a girl."

A Dominant Tomboy Masculinity

Morgan's experience in elementary and junior high school was not necessarily a disconcerting situation. Although Morgan reported that in both elementary and junior high school she had a core pack of friends who were "smart, sporty, tomboyish girls," they were actually quite popular because they participated in "all kinds of sports" and were usually the best players on the various teams. Morgan identified the following cliques in her elementary and junior high schools: "There was the popular crowd, the preppies and us tomboys and guy jocks, there were the emos and the punks, the geeks, like those in band and theater, and the nerds." Although Morgan and her tomboy friends were popular "because we were the stars on the sports teams," they often criticized the preppy girls for "putting on masks [makeup] and wearing sexy clothes trying to attract boys. We didn't like that; we saw it as stupid." Like Jessie, then, Morgan likewise felt femininity would devalue her agency and thus she constructed masculinity.

There were two competing dominant popular girls' groups in Morgan's schools—the preppies and the tomboys—and as Morgan put it, "We all knew we were different from the preppy girls, but we liked being who we were, and it never bothered us—we saw the preppy girls as the different ones." I asked Morgan what were the similarities and differences between the two groups of popular girls and she answered: "I mean for similarities we all played sports and we were all very confident in ourselves, we weren't insecure at all. But the biggest difference was we just looked different than the preppies. Like after practice and games they'd dress all sexy and we wouldn't and they had longer hair and wore makeup and we didn't. That was the major difference; plus, we were better at sports." Even though Morgan and her tomboy friends identified as girls, they drew from the boys' side of the culturally ascendant relational and discursive social structure at school in terms of gender display ("boys' clothes") and gender practice ("boys' things") yet because they were "sport stars" these tomboys were one of the dominant girl groups in her school. The duality of structure and action materialized while simultaneously there was an acceptance of the tomboys hybridized incongruence between sex and gender. Morgan therefore was practicing an in-school *dominant* tomboy masculinity.

A Localized Dominant Femininity

This competitive relationship between dominant girl groups continued throughout elementary school and into junior high, yet by the time Morgan was well into junior high school she had learned through interaction at school that "girls were supposed to be interested in boys. All over school people were all of a sudden talking about boyfriends and girlfriends and who was hooked up with who, even my tomboy friends—everyone was changing. That was the way it was; it was just what girls were expected to do." So Morgan—after numerous inner dialogues especially about wanting to fit in because she did not want to be the only tomboy—"decided that, hey, I'm a girl, right, so maybe I should act like one, act like all the other girls. And so I started to talk to my tomboy friends about clothes, makeup, growing my hair long, and stuff like that. Plus we started to talk about boys all the time, and we all started acting heterosexual by showing an interest in boys like 'Wow, he sure looks cool.' Stuff like that." I asked Morgan if she and her girlfriends were still tomboys and Morgan replied, "Oh yeah, all of us, but we started to have an interest in boys, and we started to talk about fashion stuff, so we all started to change."

Morgan's sexual awakening then—like Jessie's—began in junior high school as it was here where she initiated attaching a budding heterosexual project to her tomboy gender project, and she now seriously considered becoming more feminine. Morgan reveals negotiating here the culturally ascendant relational and discursive social structure at school that emphasized heterosexual boyfriend-girlfriend relations. And through interaction and reflexivity Morgan decided to possibly begin drawing on this structure and thus become a practicing participant within this structure.

Morgan's self-attribution as "a girl" continued to impact her re-flexivity and as such she begins to question her practiced incon-gruence between sex and gender.

A few months following the above contemplation of gender change Morgan noticed her body changing: "My breasts got a lot bigger, I started to have periods, and I started to grow taller and my hips changed." It was because of these bodily changes that Morgan began to engage in more numerous and serious inner dialogues about her changing body and "what that meant for me as a girl. I saw all my tomboy friends becoming more sexed in their bodies and more girlie in their presentation, plus my body was really changing, so I thought it was time for me to grow up and be like them, and be a real girl too." Given the changes to her body due to the onset of puberty, Morgan thought that "being a girl seemed more important now because my body changed in a very binary way. So I just started to think that I should be like my friends and so I began working on creating a very polarized gen-der presentation. I grew my hair longer and wore more feminine type of clothing and I even started to wear makeup like my friends." Morgan continued on this topic: "I was still involved in sports but after each practice and game, I now started to let my hair down, put on some makeup, and more and more girl type clothes, but I still didn't let people push me around. I went after what I wanted and I stood my ground. But I looked like all the other girls now. I guess you could say I became a preppy—we all were now!" Morgan negotiated the supplemental constraints and enablements imposed on her through bodily changes, interpret-ing these changes as meaning that she must take being a "real girl" more seriously—her sex identity—and therefore she now engaged in appropriate and thus accountable feminine display. Morgan's body constrained her from practicing tomboyism yet her body simultaneously enabled her to engage in preppy femi-nine display and social action. These developments then overlap with the discursive social structure of embodied "preppy" feminine display. Morgan drew from these conventions and they were in turn actualized through Morgan's new gendered social action and display. The duality of structure and action and congruence between sex and gender were now both materialized.

Morgan reflexively decided to "do the preppy girl thing" because her girlfriends were going through changes just as she was: her transformed body as Morgan put it "slapped me in the face." Morgan's ex-tomboy friends' bodies also changed and they subsequently began altering their hair and clothing styles, and "so we blended in with the preppies." And Morgan decided that "since I was full blown into puberty and my body became more sexed, I started to think more about my gender and feminine presentation, and I changed."

Morgan expressed to me that she came to very much enjoy entering puberty and she was "really excited about it because it was fun to dress up and be like my friends." And at the same time Morgan developed a sexual attraction toward boys. As she put it: "I was really psyched about having a developing chest and even to begin to have periods, because I saw this as now meaning that being a girl was more important than before and also that it made me more attractive. I was very good at sports, I had lotsa friends, but I still acted like I always did as a tomboy, you know, going after what I wanted, not letting people decide for me but deciding myself, being stubborn and strong. I for sure looked more feminine on the outside, but I also still acted like I always did, so that never changed."

By the time Morgan was fifteen and in high school, then, she was a hybridized "real girl" in the sense of an established congruence between sex and gender and Morgan now practiced a localized dominant preppy femininity. Morgan even began to change in terms of social action: "I had switched from sports to taking ballet lessons, and I started dating boys, and it was all great fun."

Morgan's relationship with the boys she dated always was close and friendly, yet Morgan "actually enjoyed playing computer games with them more than having sex with them." As Morgan pointed out: "I was excited about having a normal girl's body that made me more attractive. Boys were more interested in me now, and I wanted to experience heterosexuality with them and like it." During her first few years of high school, then, Morgan saw herself as a "real preppy girl" who was heterosexual and attracted to boys "like all the other girls." Morgan continued to practice stubbornness and determination "to do my own thing," and all of Morgan's friends maintained the same type of personality—these traits were incorporated into dominant preppy femininity. And Morgan as a preppy now enjoyed a steady supply of attention from boys. However, the sexuality with all of these boys "never seemed right. When we had sex, it was like I wasn't being seen. I was being interacted with in a way that didn't seem to fit. I felt like a girl, but that wasn't how I wanted to be interacted with." Morgan expressed to me that the main issue was that "they all wanted to feminize me." Morgan enjoyed being what she labeled a "strong girl" but she in no way wanted to be feminized in her behavior. As Morgan further put it: "I started to think about the way I was touched, the way I was interacted with, that it was them interacting with me, not me interacting with them. And that didn't feel like the whole story to me. I enjoyed being a girl and looking like a girl but if being a girl meant being their object then that really bothered me. So I broke up with all of them because they just treated me like an object and didn't allow me to decide how I wanted to be touched and interact sexually with them." This sexual interaction with heterosexual boys then served as a supplemental constraint and enabler in the sense of limiting Morgan's sexual agency and therefore she reflexively decided to end each relationship. This interaction also led Morgan to initiate breaking from and resisting her ongoing integration into the heterosexual relational and discursive social structure of the school.

Aligning Sex with Gender

Shortly after Morgan ended relationships with the heterosexual boys she began "hanging out" with "a gay guy" she had met in one of her high school classes, and they became "very attracted" to each other. Their attraction developed into a sexual relationship which Morgan described as "awesome." I asked Morgan how their friendship became sexual given that she identifies as straight and he identifies as gay and why that relationship was awesome. Morgan replied that "we just really hit it off. We had these great long talks about all kinds of things, and once I just kissed him because I liked him so much, and we both really liked to kiss, so we hugged and kissed some more and then ended up in bed together." Regarding the sexuality, Morgan recounted:

> He had only been with guys before, so he treated me like that. Our relationship would be defined by others as heterosexual, but it actually wasn't a heterosexual interaction with a guy. I really wasn't a girl and he didn't see me as a girl. I was the more dominant one. He actually encouraged me to be in charge, and I did. And the way we had intercourse was in the way where he was the receptive one, the energetically receptive partner and I was the energetically dominant partner, even though our anatomy was totally contradictory. And I liked it because he didn't treat me in the way other guys did, and he liked it that way too.

Morgan went on to say that the sexuality with "the gay guy" was "totally" different from her previous sexual relationships because the way the heterosexual boys interacted with her was that "I should be the submissive, feminine, receptive partner. And it totally revolutionized my ideas of how I can interact sexually with someone. I liked the way I felt with this gay guy because I was the more dominant masculine person with him, even though he was the boy and I was the girl. I was penetrating him, so it was my first experience at genderfuck." Morgan and the gay guy had several similar sexual interactions and each time Morgan felt her masculinity was further affirmed.

I asked Morgan about the nature of their desire for each other, and she responded: "I thought a lot about this, and I figured out that it was because we noticed each other's gender more than we noticed each other's sex and bodies. I was attracted to him because he was beautiful and feminine, and he was attracted to me because I was masculine in my behavior. I was a girl and he was a boy, but we ignored that and just noticed our genders." In public Morgan was a "strong girl"—which he was attracted to—but in private during sexuality she was a *masculine person* as *sex was erased* and it was this erasure that allowed the linking of her body to masculinity during sexuality. "I looked feminine but it was the sex with the gay guy where I rediscovered my masculinity. During sex with him I could be totally masculine, which I now really enjoyed again, as did he, and I didn't even think about being a girl." This particular sexual relationship then is completely re-moved from the in-school culturally ascendant heterosexual/homosexual relational and discursive social structures—as well as the in-school culturally ascendant heterosexual boyfriend/girl-friend relational and discursive social structures—and instead be-comes "queer" in the sense of being at odds with what in this setting is considered "normal" and "legitimate" sexuality and in this instance Morgan's femaleness disappears.

During her junior year of high school Morgan continued to identify as a "strong girl" yet she had inner dialogues about how much she enjoyed the "queer" sexual relationship with the gay guy—and her freedom to practice masculinity—and how much she disliked the "straight" sexual relationships with the heterosexual boys because she was feminized during those interactions. As Morgan put it, "it was the relationship with the heterosexual boys, and my experience with the gay guy, that were the catalysts in making me conscious of how I want to love and be loved, and how I want to touch and be touched and how I don't, and how I want to be in the world." These two sexual relationships then shaped Morgan's future gender *and* sexual behavior in high school. Morgan engaged in many internal conversations about these two sexual relationships and she eventually concluded that "part of my drive toward a more serious masculine gender identity was escapism and part of it was incredibly affirming. And so I don't see it as a bad thing."

Q. What do you mean by "escapism" and "affirming"?

A. It was escapism in the sense that if I'm not a pretty girl I won't be sexualized in the way the straight guys sexualized me and the gay guy didn't see me as a girl at all.

Q. So you thought if you dressed and acted masculine then you would not be attractive to heterosexual guys?

A. Exactly, that was the escapism part. I hated to be treated that way by those guys and I started to think that my femininity helped that, so I wanted to escape from that. And the affirming part was the sex with the gay guy because it actually empowered me to explore again masculinity as my gender. Sex with him was more than just sex; it was also masculine rediscovery for me. It was cool to see my masculinity affirmed, and I connected it to being a tomboy and how much I really enjoyed that.

What Morgan is identifying here is that her sexual interaction with the "gay guy"—as a supplemental constraint and enabler— empowered her to break from and begin to resist her participation in heterofemininity and its accompanying culturally ascendant relational and discursive social structures at school. Like Jessie, Morgan simultaneously refused heterofemininity—so as to avoid sexual domination by straight boys—and she once again embraced masculinity. Morgan is beginning to change her fundamental project centered on being "a girl" to viewing masculinity as more foundational, fixed, and solid—gender as primary and sex as secondary. Morgan is not quite there yet but the sexual relationship with the gay guy strongly motivated her in that direction, especially the erasure of sex during sexual interaction.

When Morgan was seventeen years old and now a senior in high school the gay guy introduced her to and she began to "hang out" with LGBT students at her high school "because I just found them to be more interesting. They were smart and artistic, and I liked that, so I stopped hanging out with my straight friends." And as with Jessie, Morgan found that her new friends emphasized gender and sexual diversity rather than dichotomy. Morgan told me that through interactions and discussions with members of this small (seven students) LGBT group that they supported her position on "escapism" and "affirming" noted above. Nevertheless, Morgan found herself in a quandary: "I couldn't get out of the binary thought pattern of being a girl, even though my LGBT friends were telling me that if I enjoyed being masculine during sex with the gay guy I must be a dude, and if I was a tomboy and I really liked being masculine, I must be a dude." Morgan had "real intense discussions" with her LGBT friends because they asserted that if Morgan had been a tomboy, if she really enjoyed being a tomboy, and if she liked to be the masculine one during sex, then she must be "a dude." These conversations with her LGBT friends—as supplemental constraints and enablers—created a predicament for Morgan that centered on her body—"I'm a girl but my LGBT friends are saying I must be a dude because how much I enjoy being masculine." And it was this contradiction that consumed much of Morgan's internal conversations at this time: "It was being a girl or a dude that kept going over and over in my head again and again that bothered me because at the same time I thought I was a girl but my friends said I must be a dude." Following extensive internal conversations, Morgan determined that "being called female felt not exactly accurate because I no longer felt like I was a girl. And at the same time I wanted to stay away from heterosexual guys, and one way to do that was to become male and emphasize my masculinity. But at the same time I thought, 'Well, if I become male and grow up, will I end up masculine like the straight guys?' So I had all this stuff going around in my head." In other words, Morgan faced an extremely complicated and contradictory dilemma.

And as with Jessie, sexuality had a major impact on Morgan's sex and gender development because "a significant part of my gender exploration was the sexuality with the gay guy. It was like I found this very affirming thing, but if it meant developing like the straight guys then it also happens to be something I hate. So it took me awhile to be comfortable being called 'he,' because 'he' was not a good thing in my mind, you know; 'he' was the straight guys." I then asked Morgan how she resolved this dilemma:

> In the end I decided that I wanted to be more complete. I didn't feel right having a girl's body because it didn't feel complete. And also I worked out that I will never really be like the straight guys if I transition. So I decided that I wanted to transition by having breast surgery and start taking hormones, then I want to do it before I go to college so that I have a name and a sex and a gender.

Morgan then points out how she decided to align her sex with her gender:

> I started binding my chest first, I stopped wearing makeup, I shaved my head, and of course just wore boys' clothes. I talked

> more with my LGBT friends about chest surgery and hor-
> mones and the two transguys in the group presented them-
> selves as "someone living the dream," which gave me permis-
> sion to investigate it more. And I started to think that stuff like
> binding was just a band-aid solution, not the real me because I
> always had to take off the band-aid. And I thought about how
> much I enjoyed being a tomboy and really enjoying being mas-
> culine and how much I enjoyed my gender presentation dur-
> ing sex with the gay guy, and hated the way I was treated by
> the straight guys, but I would never be a guy like that, so I
> decided I wanted a male body.

As a result of Morgan's interaction and conversations—as supplemental constraints and enablers—with the LGBT group in her
high school, as well as her reflexive deliberations on the dilemma
and contradiction noted above, Morgan's masculinity came to be
experienced as a disembodied event. During the summer after
high school Morgan therefore ultimately decided to transition to
male: she had breast surgery, she began to take male hormones,
and she now commenced using male pronouns (which I honor
henceforth). Morgan's parents and friends all supported his decision and as he put it, by aligning his body (sex) with masculinity
(gender) "I now felt totally complete," his masculinity was now
embodied. And masculinity (gender) now was primary in terms of
his fundamental identity and he changed his body (sex) to align
with his masculinity. This change resulted in congruence between
his sex and gender, there existed duality between structure and
action in the broader school setting, and his previous gender construction now disappeared.

A Localized Stealth Masculinity

When Morgan entered college he was "a dude" and he continued
to take hormones for the next three years. Morgan was easily
recognized as a male, as in this example: "I washed dishes as a

part-time job while in college and worked with only guys, and not one of them suspected I wasn't male." I asked Morgan what type of masculinity he constructed, and this question led to the following dialogue:

It was all about being totally stealth—a straight guy who dated women. I wanted to be male in the way masculinity is portrayed in everyday life, I wanted to be a "pop culture male," you know, the everyday guy. And I found that to pass, I had to adopt a certain kind of imagery that people associate with being that everyday guy.

Q. What do you mean by that?

A. Well, I passed as a straight male, and I had all the right mannerisms, my voice had changed, and I would strut around, you know, like young, twenty-year-old guys do, and I talked with guys about sports, girls, and stuff.

Q. So you were completely comfortable with your masculinity?

A. Not totally because I was always afraid other guys would find out that I wasn't totally male. And it bothered me that even though I was easily passing, I still felt I was constructing a feminine maleness.

Q. What do you mean by feminine maleness?

A. If you apply male standards to me, I'm way less masculine than if you apply female standards to me. You know, I was short, didn't have a penis, but still, I did easily pass as male. I was stealth.

Q. So what did you do?

A. I started to get advice from the transguys I knew as a form of "skill share," which was well intentioned. They would suggest what they found helped them pass better and feel more comfortable as a male, like "a good haircut will really help you pass." And it's true. I found that the more mainstream I looked the easier it was to pass and [the] less people would question me.

Q. Did you take any gender studies courses in college?

A. I didn't, but my friends did. My major was biology so not enough time to take other courses.

Q. So did you have trans friends in college?

A. Oh yeah, some of my LGBT friends from high school and I met a new group of friends as well. All my friends were trans in some way. I completely broke off ties with people I hung with before I transitioned.

Q. And your trans friends taught you how to "pass"?

A. For sure. They taught me all about packing, and even STPs, how to gain more muscle in my upper arms, how to walk like a guy, and where to even put my hands and stuff, like in my pockets!

Morgan learned how to become a "popular culture male" and also noted that "the hormones made me look more masculine on the outside and I often would watch my transguy friends in public and learn from them, and I'd practice what they did in front of a mirror at home. And so all this helped me to more confidently pass as a male." Morgan continued on this topic:

> The more I passed on the outside—facial hair, lower voice—
> and the more I did what the trans guys taught me, the less I

had to police my presentation. Once my voice dropped and my bone structure changed and my face changed and I had a short beard and I got my demeanor right, people never questioned if I was born female because I more easily passed. So I became more confident and I now identified as male, and I dated women who identified as straight and who were very feminine. So I applied cultural concepts in a very binary heterosexual way. And I always did the masculine things our culture says that guys do, I mimicked and mirrored those actions and experiences. The straight women I was with were all traditionally feminine and acted like an accessory to me. They were my ornaments, trimmings to my masculinity, and they would masculinize me and refer to my body in a masculine way. And that was really affirming in my transition, to hear my body referred to in masculine terms and to have beautiful straight women at my side. And I liked being with straight women because sexually they only knew how to be with guys, and so the way they would touch or talk about my body or interact with me was very much as if I was a guy.

Morgan distinguishes between "transguys" and (real) "guys" and is attempting to enter into the (real) "guy" category. Morgan draws on the culturally ascendant heteromasculine/feminine relational and discursive social structures and was now accountable as a straight "guy" who reproduced the heteronormative emphasis on male equals masculinity equals desire for females; he constructed what he labeled a "stealth masculinity" or a straight masculine maleness. Although Morgan never lived with a straight woman, he did have numerous short-term sexual relationships with such women and his localized stealth masculinity was bolstered through these particular sexual interactions:

The sexuality with these straight women was equal as we both were "top" and "bottom"—nobody dominated—and we were equally sexually satisfied, but it was a straight relationship. And that's the way I wanted it because these straight women would refer to my clitoris as "a cock" and the women would give me "blow jobs"—and I would have oral sex with them too!—and my cock is large enough now because of the "T" for us to have intercourse. And I would penetrate them and they would have these great orgasms and that was really affirming because I needed to hear that and perform that way to be comfortable with my sex and gender.

Q. Sexuality became a way to confirm your masculinity?

A. It was one of the ways for sure because I was a stealth dude and the women I had sex with made me feel masculine through and through. But it wasn't the only way. I passed in the everyday world and that was confirming.

Q. But being with feminine straight women was very important to you, right?

A. For sure, because being with feminine straight women who saw me as a man and as masculine and reflected that back to me was an incredibly necessary part of my transition. And the more I was seen with feminine looking straight women, the easier it was to pass. I was the man, and they were the girl. It was a total transition.

Morgan did not feel it was a "total transition" with all the straight women he had sex with, which is revealed in the following dialogue:

Q. Did all straight women you were with affirm your maleness and masculinity?

A. Not all. Some didn't.

Q. Why not?

A. Mainly because I didn't have a penis.

Q. Can you tell me more about that?

A. Yeah sure, some just wanted more penetration than I could give. They were really nice about it but we just didn't see each other again. And that did bother me, because when it happened it made me feel less of a man, you know, less masculine. I felt like I couldn't satisfy them, so that hurt.

Q. How did you meet these straight women?

A. We would just meet in a bar or club and then meet again for dinner, see a movie or whatever, and then have sex. It was like normal dating, you know, and we'd do it a couple times and if it didn't work out then we just didn't see each other again and we moved on.

Q. How about the other straight women?

A. They loved me. We would go on fun dates and they liked what I had for a cock, and some weren't that interested in penetration—some just liked me having oral sex with them and they enjoyed giving me blow jobs. Some liked oral sex in combination with penetration. So it was fine and I had some long-term relationships with a few of them. But it still was always there in the back of my mind that I didn't have a "real cock," and that always kinda bothered me.

Morgan engaged in relationships with certain straight women—those who affirmed his masculinity—because during sexual interaction they erased anything female about him and in turn validated Morgan's male body and embodied masculinity. These particular straight women nullified any notion of disembodied masculinity and Morgan thus transformed how both sex and mas-

culinity are constructed. Nevertheless, Morgan experienced masculine insecurity—even with the "affirming women"—because he
did not possess a "real penis." In other words, not possessing a
"real penis" constituted a challenge to Morgan's masculinity—
feelings of disembodiment continually reappeared.

Q. Did not having a penis pose as a challenge to your stealth
masculinity?

A. For sure, because some of the straight women I had sex
with didn't want to see me again and they were always women
who the sex didn't go that great with, and that bothered me
because I thought I didn't measure up, you know, like I didn't
have a real penis, you know, so that's why the sex didn't go that
well.

Q. But many straight women enjoyed sex with you?

A. Oh yeah, it just kinda bothered me, not having a real penis,
you know. Like I said, that was always in the back of my mind.

Despite enjoying being a "stealth dude" and having relationships with certain straight women, the issue of "not having a real
penis" considerably distressed Morgan. His body now posed as a
supplemental constraint on his transition to male and thus established a significant challenge to his masculinity. Seemingly unable
to always construct difference during sexuality, incongruence between sex and gender materialized. And simultaneously some of
the transguys at college would ask Morgan to share stories, like
"'when was the first time I knew I was trans' and coming out
stories." Morgan's transguy friends frequently gave him advice on
how to pass but "a select few" often questioned him about his
past. For example, "they would ask me when I first knew I liked
'male stuff,' like baseball, and when I realized I really liked girls.
And I thought—but I didn't tell them—yeah, that's part of it, but

I also loved to do ballet, I was psyched about my developing breasts, I really liked being a girl and going through puberty, and I dated boys and had sex with them." Morgan "learned from these transguys to selectively narrate, to pull out the pieces of my history that correspond to being male and leave behind the rest—the female and feminine stuff." Morgan then went along with what he labeled the "trans narrative" by emphasizing parts of his history that evidenced a transman sex and gender while simultaneously eschewing all the feminine parts of his past.

Neither Masculine *nor* Feminine

After further extensive and careful internal conversations Morgan began to question his transition and his construction of a stealth masculinity. As Morgan put it: "I realized that a large part of my history was lost and so I attempted to rediscover those parts I left behind, by looking through family albums and examining pictures of my life as a girl, and I started to take that part of me back." Morgan went on to point out: "I realized that to be a stealth dude I had to reconstruct my entire childhood in order to have a history that doesn't sound weird when I talk about it. So when I interacted with a few of the transguys, I couldn't say, 'Oh, I did ballet and dated these dudes.' I was creating an entire new history of myself. And part of me now—which is post-dude—is remembering and putting all the pieces together to make one cohesive person that had had all these experiences. So now I'm in a new transition." Here Morgan is revealing his break from and resistance to what he labels the "trans narrative" as a culturally significant discursive social structure amongst his trans friends, and so I asked Morgan to be more specific as to how this new transition came about:

> Well, one night I decided to look at my entire naked body in a full-length mirror, and I didn't really recognize myself. And I

said, "Oh shit." And I realized I had gone too far. I saw my face and the top of my body as male, but the bottom part was female because I didn't have a penis. But I was afraid to share this with my trans friends. So I tried to ignore it as much as I could. And then one of my transguy friends shared his experience with me. He had just come off of hormones because he decided transition was not for him. And we talked a lot about this and he didn't have a penis either and he like me couldn't afford phalloplasty and then seeing his change and having that permission and that modeling of that experience was so cool. And so I interpreted this as finally seeing the last piece. And I told him how much I liked our talks and he said he really liked talking with me, and we became very close. And then he and I had a wonderful same-sex sexual experience, because our bodies were the same—we both had chest surgery and took hormones—so we truly were the same sex but not your traditional male or female, but still the same. So it was these thoughts and that sexual experience that led me to think I was genderqueer and not trans.

This supplemental constraint and enabler in the form of conversations and a "queer" sexual experience were crucial in motivating Morgan to realize that "I'm not straight because even if I'm attracted to straight women and we interacted as male-female and masculine-feminine, I was not afforded the same permissions as regular straight men." Morgan came to understand after much reflexivity (during and after the above same-sex relationship) "that my relationship with straight women was more of a genderqueer experience, not a culturally straight relationship. And there was always the risk that the straight women would be with a straight dude, and in that sense our relationship was not straight. Some of the straight women were real nice and didn't seem to care that I didn't have a real penis, but I didn't feel right, you know, it always seemed to go back to that I didn't have a real cock. So I decided I must be genderqueer, flexible, fluid, nonstraight. And this was the case for both gender and sexuality." The conversation and sexual experience noted above—as well as the physiology of his body—enabled Morgan to question his transition to male: "I started questioning the next stage of transition, a hysterectomy and phalloplasty, and I thought how expensive they were and how phalloplasty doesn't usually work and how a hysterectomy will permanently end my chance of transitioning back. Plus I started thinking about being chemically dependent upon 'T' for the rest of my life. And then I got this thought that I may want to have children at some point. And so I decided I'm not having a hysterectomy because someday I'm going to carry a child, and I then stopped taking hormones." This disconnect from the "trans narrative" allowed Morgan to "look at my past and revisit pieces that got pushed to the wayside in the hope of expressing this one piece, which happens to be my masculinity. And so the feminine part of me was lost, and that was a great sadness for me because that important part of me became invisible."

Morgan began to reconnect with his feminine past and he asked himself, "What did I like to do as a girl?" After reflexively thinking about this question, Morgan realized that much of his *self* had been erased:

> I was on hormones for three years, and I saw it as giving up a part of myself to adhere to the script. So I started to deconstruct my history and rediscover my feminine past. And I realized how much I didn't like being a stealth dude just as I didn't like being a stealth chick from age 13 to 17. So it was about going back in my history and finding the pieces that made up the whole story. It was like opening a treasure chest that I locked away. All the answers are in that chest that holds the other parts of myself. So it's a whole new transition and coming out process by embracing parts of me that I haven't had in a long time.

Morgan described himself now as possessing "all traits of gender and it's not so much a matter of breaking down specific behaviors as looking at feelings that generate behaviors. I'm neither masculine nor feminine so I don't pass as anything, I don't hype up on one side or the other—I have synthesized everything, and I always use, and ask other people to use, gender-neutral pronouns," in particular "ze" and "zir." Morgan went on to point out that ze does not "consciously try to act gendered in any specific way, and others have a hard time reading me as either male or female. People are confused all the time." I asked Morgan why people had a hard time reading zir as expressing a particular gender and ze responded, "Because I have so many bodies and so many past experiences all wrapped into one—a tomboy, a straight female-bodied person, a masculine female-bodied male, a female-to-male transman, and a genderqueer person—which is a very different gender than being born female and always being female and acting feminine."

Morgan explained the "genderqueer person" in the following way: "It's when I rediscovered my feminine past, but when I did that, it's not really going back to femininity as it is going forward to something new. It's like I'm queering queer! So I feel and act many genders based on this history of different bodies and genders. And if I'm many genders then I'm neither masculine nor feminine." Morgan offered this example: "If I'm in a gay bar, some guys will read me as an effeminate guy, and others will read me as a transwoman, and dykes will read me as a transguy or as a butch dyke. I have a lot of different genders just standing there having a drink. I encompass so much, but I'm very fixed in who I am." Becoming genderqueer, then, is a hybridized gender construction for Morgan.

At the time of the interview Morgan was in a relationship with "a female-bodied person and we both are pansexual. We are fluid in our sexuality as sometimes I'm the dominant one, the more masculine, and sometimes she is. So we change roles—our sexuality is up, down, and all over bodies. It's always changing. We've engaged in every sexual position in the book, and then some. And now that I'm genderqueer, it doesn't actually matter what my body looks like. My body is in between."

Q. So your body now fits well with your genderqueer identity?

A. Yeah, for sure. I don't have a male or a female body, and that's what fits me. I don't have breasts but I have a vagina, so I'm neither.

Morgan identifies as genderqueer because "being born female gave me a certain set of experiences, and then transitioning to male gave me more experiences, and then adding back in my femaleness gave me kind of a postmodern gender transition. An identity implies experience, and really I've had far more experiences than one identity can encompass. So yeah, I'm genderqueer because my identity expresses many genders in a multifaceted way."

I asked Morgan how masculinity now fit into this genderqueer identity:

> Like I said earlier, I don't attempt to pass or act in any special gender way, but some people read me as a straight masculine guy, some as a feminine guy, some as a transman or transwoman, and some as a masculine female. It is difficult to categorize me because I entail so many genders. Masculinity is there if you want to see it, but so are many other genders. You can't say I'm just one gender. It is kind of like the color white, which is really the full spectrum of colors, even though it would be identified as the absence of color. That's what I mean. So if you were to highlight and look at part of that spectrum, you could pull out the red value, or the blue value, or the green value, in full spectrum light, but to the naked eye it just seems to have nothing. So if you wanted to look at the masculine part of my identity, you could find it, but it's together with other

parts in a space that is usually seen as nothing, like the color white.

Let us now turn to chapter 5 where I discuss the two most recent U.S. presidents and their regional and global hegemonic masculinities as well as their global dominating masculinities.

5

PRESIDENTS: BUSH AND OBAMA

In chapters 3 and 4 I examined how Sam, Jerry, Jessie, and Morgan drew on and reproduced—yet at times broke from and resisted—relational social structures that concurrently proffered meaningful discursive representations (as an overlapping social structure) through embodied appearance and practice. Chapter 5 shifts the analysis to how the two most recent U.S. presidents drew from and reproduced (in new form) a discursive social structure that concurrently embeds unequal gender relations (as an overlapping social structure) metaphorically and thus symbolically. In other words, through their speechifying both presidents engaged in communicative social action constituted by intersecting discursive and relational social structures.

Following the September 11, 2001, terrorist attacks on the World Trade Center towers in New York City and the Pentagon building in Washington, DC, U.S. president George W. Bush (henceforth Bush) immediately determined that to "defend freedom" he must launch a "global war on terror," initially against Afghanistan, then against Iraq. After militarily assaulting Afghanistan and removing the Taliban from power for harboring Al Qaida and Osama bin Laden, Bush turned his military attention to Iraq because Saddam Hussein allegedly both threatened the entire "civilized" world with weapons of mass destruction and maintained a deep connection to international terrorists.

Shortly after being elected U.S. president Barack Obama (henceforth, Obama) announced in 2009 that the major consequence of Bush's war against Iraq was the removal of the military's focus on the "real" global war on terror against Al Qaida in Afghanistan (2009a; 2009b). Obama emphasized that such attention to Iraq and subsequent inattention to Afghanistan provided the occasion for Al Qaida and the Taliban to regroup and begin again their terrorist activity in Afghanistan as well as Pakistan. Obama proposed that the United States deepen its commitment to defeating Al Qaida and the Taliban in Afghanistan and Pakistan. On December 1, 2009, Obama declared that he would order a unilateral preemptive U.S. military surge in Afghanistan and Pakistan allegedly to prevent a new "safe haven" for Al Qaida and therefore future terrorist attacks against the world (2009c).

Subsequently, and as pointed out in the introduction, in that same year (2009) I decided to examine *all* of Bush's speeches (public addresses) that focused on Iraq from January 29, 2002, to the U.S.-led military invasion on March 19, 2003. And most recently I have concentrated on and examined Obama's speeches that centered on Afghanistan from January 20, 2009, to December 31, 2014.

In preparing their speeches both presidents drew on the villain-victim-hero culturally significant discursive social structure and each subsequently through their individual sets of speeches framed a new discourse emphasizing a metaphorical and unequal relationship among protective hegemonic masculinity, emphasized femininity, and subordinate masculinity. Both presidents' speeches in total contributed to the deployment of a discursive social structure legitimating regionally and globally gendered inequality as well as framing a rationale for military force against Iraq and Afghanistan. But in addition, this gender hegemony—

which discursively sanctions the global war on terror—is supplemented by global dominating masculine practices that include torture, secret detention, and extraordinary rendition (by Bush) and extrajudicial executions (by Obama).

I begin the discussion with Bush.

BUSH

The content analysis indicated that Bush fashioned himself through his speeches as *the* hegemonic masculine heroic protector of the "civilized" people of the world from the "uncivilized" terroristic Saddam Hussein. Furthermore, Bush supplemented this protector image with a rescuer hegemonic masculinity in order to justify his military endeavor in the alleged global war on terror: an attack on Iraq. I first summarize a representative sample of the concepts and phrases used by Bush in his speeches concerning Iraq and then I turn to his involvement in torture, secret detention, and extraordinary rendition.

A Regional and Global *Protector/Rescuer* Hegemonic Masculinity

Throughout his speeches Bush constructed then president of Iraq Saddam Hussein as an uncivilized, toxically masculine metaphoric *villain*, bent on violence, terror, and the oppression and repression of his people. Bush repeatedly described Saddam Hussein as a "homicidal dictator" who is "skilled in the techniques of deception," who is "addicted to weapons of mass destruction," and who is a "torturer," a "tyrant," a "terrorist," and a "murderer" (2002e; 2002f). For Bush, "Saddam's" evilness is embedded in his "nature," resulting in opponents being "decapitated and their heads displayed outside their homes," women being "systematically raped," "political prisoners made to watch their own children being tortured," and "Saddam" sending "other people's children on missions of suicide and murder" (2002a). In short, "Iraq is ruled by perhaps the world's most brutal dictator who already has committed genocide," who "embraces tyranny and death as cause and creed," and who maintains "ruthless ambition, unconstrained by law or morality"—he is therefore the quintessential metaphoric toxically masculine *villain,* and because of his evil and uncivilized nature, "Saddam Hussein is a threat to our peace" (2002a; 2002b; 2002c; 2002d; 2002e).

Bush declared that this naturally evil and villainous dictator had weapons of mass destruction at his disposal, together with strong ties to international terrorist networks, all of which inflated the essence of his threat. Bush underlined that this combination of ties to international terrorist groups and the "stockpiling" of weapons of mass destruction created an acute situation whereby the "civilized world" was faced with "unprecedented dangers" (2002a). Accordingly, Bush constantly underlined that "while there are many dangers in the world, the threat from Iraq stands alone because it gathers the most serious dangers of our age in one place," and that the danger of "past and present actions" only "grows worse with time. If we know Saddam Hussein has dangerous weapons today—and we do—does it make any sense for the world to wait to confront him as he grows even stronger and develops even more dangerous weapons?" (2002e). Saddam Hussein was not simply a major threat to "American" men, women, and children, but to all "civilized" people throughout the world. Bush (2002b) further emphasized that "the terror that targeted New York and Washington could next strike any center of civilization." Because the entire "civilized world" was a possible victim, that world must be protected so as to "deliver our children from a future of fear," and so that the "civilized" worldwide citizenry could choose "human choice against coercion and cruelty" and "lawful change against chaotic violence" (2002b). Bush

(2002a; 2002e) "will not wait on events, while dangers gather. I will not stand by, as peril draws closer and closer," and will not "ignore the threat gathering against us. Facing clear evidence of peril, we cannot wait for the final proof, the smoking gun, that could come in the form of a mushroom cloud"—"I will not relent in this struggle for the freedom and security of my own country and the civilized world" (2002b). Thus the "entire civilized world" also was metaphorically designated *probable victims* of Saddam Hussein's future terror who were in need of *protection* from Bush.

In addition to emphasizing that "Saddam Hussein's regime was a grave and gathering danger" to "Americans" and the "civilized" men, women, and children around the world (2002b), Bush (2002c; 2002d) highlighted the suffering that "the world's most brutal dictator" inflicts "on his own people." Bush further pointed out that Iraqi men, women, and children "are the daily victims of Saddam Hussein's oppression": he "has used weapons of death against innocent Iraqi people," and has "committed genocide with chemical weapons, ordered the torture of children, and instituted the systematic rape of the wives and daughters of his political opponents" (2002c; 2002d). In short, Saddam Hussein was involved in the "persecution" of Iraq's entire "civilian population," thereby turning "Iraq into a prison, a poison factory, and a torture chamber for patriots and dissidents" (2002e; 2003a). Consequently, Iraqi men, women, and children became metaphorical *victims* in need of *rescue* by Bush.

This story of an evil, uncivilized, toxically masculine metaphorical villain inevitably attacking "American" and other "civilized" men, women, and children of the world, as well as oppressing and repressing Iraqi men, women, and children, constitutes discursively the reason for responding militarily and preemptively against Iraq. As Bush often put it: "we cannot leave the future of peace and the security" of the "civilized world" and the Iraqi people "in the hands of this cruel and dangerous man. The dictator must be disarmed" (2002d). To protect the "civilized world" from this dangerous and villainous threat, Bush metaphorically painted himself regionally and globally as the *hegemonic masculine heroic protector* by "confronting the threat posed by Iraq" as "crucial to winning the war on terror. Those who harbor terrorists are as guilty as the terrorists themselves" because "terror cells and outlaw regimes building weapons of mass destruction are different faces of the same evil" (2002e). Bush would lead the protection of "Americans" and the "civilized world" from "terror networks of global reach"; the United States of America "has never permitted the brutal and lawless to set history's course"; therefore, it became his "urgent duty" to protect not simply "Americans," but "other lives, without illusion and without fear" (2002b; 2002d; 2002e).

In addition to protecting "Americans" and other "civilized" men, women, and children from the terror of Saddam Hussein, Bush stated he would also rescue the Iraqi people from their brutal dictator. Bush (2003b) made clear that he "will tear down the apparatus of terror" and help the Iraqi people "build a new Iraq that is prosperous and free. In a free Iraq, there will be no more wars of aggression against your neighbors, no more poison factories, no more executions of dissidents, no more torture chambers and rape rooms. The tyrant soon will be gone. The day of your liberation is near." To Bush (2002h), Iraqi men, women, and children had "suffered too long in silent captivity. Liberty for the Iraqi people is a great moral cause." Once Bush had disarmed Saddam Hussein, "the first and greatest benefit will come to Iraqi men, women, and children," the "oppression of Kurds, Assyrians, Turkomans, Shi'a, Sunnis, and others will be lifted," and "the long captivity of Iraq will end, and an era of new hope will begin" (2002e). In short, "the time has come for the Iraqi people to escape oppression, find freedom, and live in hope," and through

Bush's efforts "the people of Iraq can shake off their captivity"; he "will give the Iraqi people their chance to live in freedom and choose their own Government"; he will help the "Iraqis achieve a unified, stable, and free country"; and he will do so with "no ambition in Iraq except to remove a threat and restore control of that country to its own people" (2002d; 2002g; 2003a; 2003c). Bush then constructed himself regionally and globally as the metaphorical *hegemonic masculine heroic rescuer* who would liberate Iraqi men, women, and children from their oppression as well as oversee their journey to freedom.

Bush (2002e) summarized his protection/rescue strategy regarding Iraq as follows:

> We did not ask for this present challenge, but we accept it. Like other generations of Americans, we will meet the responsibility of defending human liberty against violence and aggression. By our resolve, we will give strength to others. By our courage, we will give hope to others. And by our actions, we will secure the peace and lead the world to a better day.

Given Bush's unique "understanding of the threats of our time, and the designs and deceptions of the Iraqi regime," he consequently had "an urgent duty to prevent the worst from occurring" (2002e). If Bush "fails to act," it would "embolden other tyrants," allow "terrorists access to new weapons and new resources," and make "blackmail a permanent feature of world events"; through inaction, "the United States would resign itself to a future of fear," and "that is not the America I know. That is not the America I serve. We refuse to live in fear. Now, as before, we will secure our Nation, protect our freedom," and act so that "millions" throughout the world do not "live or die at the discretion of a brutal dictator. That's not true peace, and we won't accept it" (2002e; 2002f).

Bush emphasized that he does *not* "desire to see military conflict" because he "values life and never seeks war unless it is essential to security and justice"—"Hopefully, this can be done peacefully" (2002c; 2002f). Bush is "doing everything" he can "to avoid war in Iraq," yet he "must be willing to use military force," but he will enter "into battle" only "as a last resort" (2002f; 2003b). For Bush, then, he "enters this conflict reluctantly," and although "every measure has been taken to avoid war," once entered "every measure will be taken to win it" (2003b; 2003c). It is *only by necessity* that "America" will become aggressive against Iraq, as aggression is the "only certain means of removing a great danger" to "all civilized nations" (2002e), and Bush "will see to it that this judgment is enforced" (2002i).

Accordingly, on March 17, 2003, Bush (2003b) announced that "Saddam Hussein and his sons must leave Iraq within 48 hours. Their refusal to do so will result in military conflict, commenced at a time of our choosing." Given that Saddam Hussein and his sons did not leave Iraq within the 48-hour deadline, on March 19, 2003, Bush launched a military attack against Iraq. "The only way to limit its duration," Bush declared, "is to apply decisive force. And I assure you, this will not be a campaign of half measures, and we will accept no outcome but victory" (2003c).

A GLOBAL DOMINATING MASCULINITY

In addition to the above regional and global protector/rescuer hybrid tough and tender hegemonic masculinity, Bush constructed a global dominating masculinity, which I turn to in this section. This global dominating masculinity involved torture, secret detention, and extraordinary rendition. For example, the U.S. *Inquiry into the Treatment of Detainees in U.S. Custody* report (Committee on Armed Services, 2008) concludes in part that the Bush administration actually applied relentless pressure on U.S. interrogators (at prisons in Guantánamo Bay, Cuba; in Afghanistan and Iraq; and in various "black sites" around the globe) to use torture techniques on detainees in order to force false confessions signaling a link between Al Qaida and Saddam Hussein (and thus support for Bush's communicative social action discussed above). For example, Colonel Lawrence Wilkerson (2009), former chief of staff of the Department of State during the term of Secretary of State Colin Powell, states that the Bush administration authorized such "harsh interrogations" for the purpose of in part "discovering a smoking gun linking Iraq and Al Qaida" (p. 2). Wilkerson (p. 2) states further that "so furious was this effort that on one particular detainee, even when the interrogation team had reported . . . that their detainee 'was compliant' (meaning the team recommended no more torture), the [White House] ordered them to continue the enhanced methods" because the "detainee had not yet revealed any Al Qaida-Baghdad contacts." And most recently Wilkerson (2014: 4) pointed out that he learned in April 2002—approximately one year prior to the onset of the Iraq War and seven months after 9/11—that the torture interrogation techniques "were as much aimed at Al Qaida and contacts between Baghdad and Al Qaida, and corroboration thereof, as they were trying to ferret out whether or not there was another attack coming, like 9/11. That was stunning to me to find out that that was 50 percent of the impetus."

According to the Committee on Armed Services numerous former senior U.S. intelligence officers reported that throughout 2002 and 2003 the White House demanded proof from interrogators of a link between Al Qaida and Iraq. And it was during this same time period that two alleged top Al Qaida officials were repeatedly tortured through "waterboarding" (immobilizing the detainee in an inclined position and then pouring water over the breathing passages so as to induce an experience of drowning through a gag reflex): Abu Zubaydah was waterboarded 83 times in August 2002 and Khalid Sheikh Mohammed 183 times in March 2003. And former U.S. Army psychiatrist Major Paul Burney reported to the committee the following about his experiences of such interrogations at the Guantánamo Bay, Cuba, prison (p. 41):

> While we were there a large part of the time we were focused on trying to establish a link between Al Qaida and Iraq and we were not successful in establishing a link between Al Qaida and Iraq. The more frustrated people got in not being able to establish that link . . . there was more and more pressure to resort to measures that might produce more immediate results.

Burney (p. 50) goes on to point out that there existed "increasing pressure to get 'tougher' with detainee interrogations" and that "a lot of pressure to use more coercive techniques" was frequent. And according to the recent Senate Select Committee on Intelligence (2014) executive summary of torture committed during the rendition, detention, and interrogation program, this get "tougher" approach included forced feedings, both orally and anally (rectal rehydration); threats to rape and murder the children of family members of prisoners; compulsory standing for hours on foot and ankle injuries; threats with guns and power drills; mock executions; coerced sleep deprivation for up to 180 hours (over one week) resulting in "disturbing" hallucinations; placing prisoners in coffin-sized boxes for up to eleven days; prisoners compelled to stand with their hands over their head for up to 54 hours; forced nudity; up to twenty days of nonstop "enhanced interrogation techniques"; prisoners refused access to toilets, put in diapers, and left hanging by their wrists for extended periods of time; prisoners shackled for hours in stress positions; and ice baths. And the Committee on Armed Services report concluded that support for these torture practices came from the highest levels of the White House (p. xxvi):

On February 7, 2002, President George W. Bush made a written determination that Common Article 3 of the Geneva Conventions, which would have afforded minimum standards for humane treatment, did not apply to Al Qaida or Taliban detainees. Following the President's determination, techniques such as waterboarding, nudity, and stress positions . . . were authorized for use in interrogations of detainees in U.S. custody.

The same report also noted that members of the President's Cabinet discussed specific interrogation techniques inside the White House, National Security Council members reviewed the CIA's interrogation program, and members of the Justice Department's Office of Legal Counsel wrote legal opinions that "distorted the meaning and intent of anti-torture laws, rationalized the abuse of detainees in U.S. custody, and influenced Department of Defense determinations as to what interrogation techniques were legal for use during interrogations conducted by U.S. military personnel" (pp. xxvi–xxvii).

In an analysis of recently declassified CIA documents, it was found that the CIA leadership knew that their agency's involvement in "enhanced interrogation techniques" was "wrong" and they therefore never felt "fully confident that the authorization [the CIA] received from the executive branch was enough," so they continually asked for approval to treat detainees in a cruel and inhumane manner (Cole, 2015: 5). And as these documents show, such official White House permission came from the president, the vice president, the attorney general, the national security adviser, and senior lawyers in each of these offices (p. 5). Accordingly, a "White House Torture Team" had been established to officially redefine and legitimize torture in the hope of in part obtaining false confessions supporting a link between Al Qaida and Iraq, all of which was camouflaged through Bush's regional and global hegemonic masculine discursive structured action (see also McCoy, 2006; Sands, 2008).

Bush formally approved these torture practices, he ordered the CIA secret detention program, he approved the program of extraordinary renditions, and he stated in his memoir that he personally selected the torture techniques that were used (Bush, 2010; Holtzman, 2012; Human Rights Watch, 2011; Open Society Foundations, 2013). The secret detention program involved suspected terrorists held in CIA prisons in "black sites" around the globe and during their detention subjected to torture and the extraordinary rendition program encompassed transferring a detainee (without any legal process) to a prison in a foreign country for the purpose of detention and torture (Open Society Foundations, 2013).

As the recent Open Society Foundations (2013: 5) report *Globalizing Torture* concludes: "The two programs entailed the abduction and disappearance of detainees and their extralegal transfer on secret flights to undisclosed locations around the world, followed by their incommunicado detention, interrogation, torture, and abuse." The report (p. 6) makes clear the *global* nature of the torture, secret detention, and extraordinary rendition program approved by Bush, documenting at least fifty-four foreign governments' participation in a variety of ways, including hosting CIA prisons inside their borders; detaining, interrogating, torturing, and abusing individuals; assisting in the capture and transport of detainees; permitting use of domestic airspace and airports for secret flights transporting detainees; and providing intelligence leading to secret detention and extraordinary rendition of individuals. Without the participation of these governments, then, the secret detention and extraordinary rendition operations—and their accompanying torture—could not have been accomplished.

Bush's leadership practices involving torture, secret detention, and extraordinary renditions constitute a global dominating masculinity because he commanded and controlled the particular interactions associated with decisions about each, he exercised power and control over people and events: he was "calling the shots" and "running the show," but he is not legitimating unequal relations between men and women, masculinity and femininity.

I now turn to Obama.

OBAMA

The content analysis of Obama's speeches on Afghanistan indicate that he likewise fashioned himself as *the* hegemonic masculine heroic protector of American, Afghan, and all citizens of the NATO alliance countries from the terroristic emissaries of "evil": the Taliban and Al Qaida, and most recently the so-called Islamic State. Similar to Bush, Obama constructs this protector hegemonic masculinity through a villain-victim-hero narrative to justify his continuance of the alleged global war on terror through a military attack on the Taliban and Al Qaida in Afghanistan and eventually other Middle Eastern countries. I first summarize a representative sample of the concepts and phrases used by Obama in his speeches on Afghanistan and then I turn to his involvement in extrajudicial executions.

A Regional and Global *Protector* Hegemonic Masculinity

The regional and global gendered practices of Bush set a perilous precedent for Obama and, painfully, he is on record as committed to the global war on terror through initially his Bush-style "surge" in Afghanistan and Pakistan. During his first year as president Obama became the *new* global heroic hegemonic masculine protector (but not the rescuer, like Bush) and he has continued in this position throughout his presidency. In a speech on March 27, 2009, that outlines his strategy for Afghanistan, Obama (2009a) asks the question: "What is our purpose in Afghanistan?" His answer is as follows (2009a):

Al Qaida and its allies, the terrorists who planned and supported the 9/11 attacks, are in Pakistan and Afghanistan.
Multiple intelligence estimates have warned that Al Qaida is
actively planning attacks on the United States homeland from
its safe haven in Pakistan. And if the Afghan Government falls
to the Taliban or allows Al Qaida to go unchallenged, that
country will again be a base for terrorists who want to kill as
many of our people as they possibly can.

Obama goes on to point out that a resurgent Al Qaida and
Taliban in Pakistan and/or Afghanistan "is not simply an
American problem," it is "an international security challenge of
the highest order. . . . The safety of people around the world is at
stake" (2009a). Consequently, Obama (2009a) must assume the
position of a *global heroic hegemonic masculine protector*:

> As President, my greatest responsibility is to protect the
> American people. . . . We are in Afghanistan to confront a
> common enemy that threatens the United States, our friends,
> and our allies, and the people of Afghanistan and Pakistan who
> have suffered the most at the hands of violent extremists. So I
> want the American people to understand that we have a clear
> and focused goal to disrupt, dismantle, and defeat Al Qaida in
> Pakistan and Afghanistan and to prevent their return to either
> country in the future. That's the goal that must be achieved;
> that is a cause that could not be more just. And to the terrorists
> who oppose us, my message is the same: We will defeat you.

In 2009 Obama committed 21,000 additional U.S. troops to
Afghanistan and Pakistan for the purpose of fighting Al Qaida and
the Taliban as well as to train Afghan security forces. Obama
began to trudge through the all-too-familiar foreign policy "Bush
path" in the Middle East—he endorsed through his communicative social action and other practices the global war on terror.

Throughout his speeches Obama depicted the Taliban and Al
Qaida as "far-reaching networks of violence and hatred" whose

members are "vicious and evil people" that "induce terror," "slaughter innocents," and are "determined to kill on a massive scale" throughout the world (2009d; 2009e; 2009f). For Obama, the Taliban and Al Qaida are the world's premier, "nimble," and "ruthless enemies" because "hatred lies in their heart" and consequently they "do not value human life" (2009a; 2009g). The Taliban and Al Qaida are a "contagion of extremism" whose members are "murderous and craven" and who "have no scruples and would willingly and gladly kill innocents" (2009h; 2009i; 2009j). In short, the Taliban and Al Qaida "will stop at nothing in their efforts to kill Americans" and they likewise "threaten every member of NATO" (2010c; 2009h). In Obama's speeches, then, the Taliban and Al Qaida constitute the metaphorical toxically masculine *villains*.

Obama portrayed Americans, Afghans, and all citizens of the NATO countries as "innocent" people who are thus vulnerable to terrorism because they are unable to protect themselves from the ongoing "violent extremism" of the Taliban and Al Qaida (2009k; 2009d; 2009g). For Obama, the "terrorists" are continually "plotting to harm innocent" Americans, Afghans, and all citizens of NATO countries because the Taliban and Al Qaida are "a band of men" who are so "intent on killing innocent men, women, and children" in these countries that the "safety of people around the world is at stake"—"all people are endangered" (2009g; 2010a; 2009a; 2009c). These two "terrorist groups" are "a threat to the people of Afghanistan, a threat to the people of America, but they're also a threat to people all around the world" (2010b). Americans, Afghans, and all citizens of NATO countries are not directly involved in all events related to the Taliban and Al Qaida yet they passively will possibly suffer the consequences of global terrorism unless they are properly protected. For Obama, then, these three groups were metaphorically designated the *probable victims* of the future terror perpetrated by the Taliban and Al Qaida *villains.*

This story of metaphorical, toxically masculine villains violently threatening vulnerable and innocent men, women, and children in the United States, in Afghanistan, and in all NATO countries, establishes discursively the reason for Obama's military "surge" in Afghanistan as well as all military strikes in the Middle East to follow. As Obama declared, "Our Nation is at war. We are at war against Al Qaida . . . that is plotting to strike us again. And I will do whatever it takes to defeat them" (2010c; 2010d). Obama goes on to assert that "We face a very tough fight in Afghanistan. . . . But we will not tolerate a safe haven for terrorists who want to destroy Afghan society from within and launch attacks against innocent men, women, and children in our country and around the world" (2010d). Without question, "this mission is fundamental to the ability of free people to live in peace and security in the 21st century" (2010d). To protect "free people" from the dangerous and villainous threat, Obama metaphorically represented himself in his speeches regionally and globally as the *hegemonic masculine heroic protector* who is "ready to lead" because of his knowledgeable and informed "American exceptionalism"; Obama embodies the decisiveness and therefore the ability to "confront the emerging danger" and "protect" the passively dependent and vulnerably innocent possible victims (2009d; 2009h; 2009g). As "Commander in Chief" Obama will protect the "free world" by "doing for the people what they cannot do by themselves"—he will "disrupt, dismantle, and defeat Al Qaida and its extremist allies in Afghanistan and Pakistan" and therefore "prevent their capacity to threaten America and our allies in the future" (2012a; 2010e).

Obama often stated that he has the "responsibility to do whatever is necessary" to "keep the nation safe" and the world is "waiting for us to lead" (2010f; 2009l; 2009k). The reemergence of the

Taliban and Al Qaida in Afghanistan and Pakistan allegedly creates an "international security challenge of the highest order" (2009a). And for Obama, his "greatest responsibility is to protect" and thus his "message to terrorists" is: "I will defeat you" (2009a). As Obama continues: "My goal is to destroy their [Taliban and Al Qaida] capacity to inflict harm on the U.S." as well as "on people of all faiths and all nationalities all around the world" (2009m). Obama will do "everything in my power to keep Americans and their families safe and secure," "I will leave no stone unturned in seeking better ways to protect the American people" as well as "all people around the world" (2009n; 2010a; 2010b). Consequently, Obama depicted himself regionally and globally as the metaphorical *hegemonic masculine heroic protector*.

By 2011 Obama began to announce to the world that he had been a successful hegemonically masculine protector. On May 1, 2011, Obama declared that he had orchestrated the killing of "Osama bin Laden, the leader of Al Qaida and a terrorist who's responsible for the murder of thousands of innocent men, women, and children" (2011a). For Obama, the killing (or capture) of bin Laden was "the top priority of our war against Al Qaida, even as we continued our broader efforts to disrupt, dismantle, and defeat his network . . . . The death of bin Laden marks the most significant achievement to date in our Nation's effort to defeat Al Qaida" (2011a). And by October of 2011, Obama indicated that now "our citizens are safer and our Nation is more secure" because Obama had "delivered justice to Osama bin Laden and many other Al Qaida leaders" (2011b). The military under Obama's command "pushed the Taliban out of key strongholds, Afghan security forces are growing stronger, and the Afghan people have a new chance to forge their own future" (2011b). Because of this success, "we have begun to draw down our forces in Afghanistan and transition security to the Afghan people" (2011b).

A Global Dominating Masculinity

Obama's proclamation of masculine success was at best prematature; by 2013 he acknowledged that "we still face significant challenges" in Afghanistan (2013a). Although he planned to have "most troops home" from Afghanistan by the end of 2014, there will remain a "follow-on presence of U.S. troops" that will train, assist, and advise Afghan forces and "make sure that Al Qaida and its affiliates cannot launch an attack against the United States or other countries from Afghan soil" (2013a). In addition to "significant challenges" continuing from Al Qaida and the Taliban in Afghanistan (and Pakistan), Obama disclosed: "We've seen the emergence of various Al Qaida affiliates. From Yemen to Iraq, from Somalia to North Africa, the threat today is more diffuse, with Al Qaida's affiliates in the Arabian peninsula, AQAP, the most active in plotting against our homeland" (2013b). And on September 10, 2014, Obama announced that the greatest terrorist threat now was the group known as the "Islamic State," formerly an Al Qaida affiliate, that controls (at the time this book goes to press) an increasing number of towns in western Syria and northern Iraq (2014a). Obama's (2014a) response to the "Islamic State" consisted of *toughness* through airstrikes, supporting Iraqi troops on the ground, and other counterterrorism measures, such as various forms of surveillance, as well as a bit of *tenderness* by providing humanitarian assistance to civilians who have been displaced by the "Islamic State." And in particular, this continued expansion of terror groups—rather than their contraction—involves an additional form of toughness, engaging in "a series of persistent, targeted efforts to dismantle specific networks of violent extremists," specifically through the use of "remotely piloted aircraft, commonly referred to as *drones*" (emphasis added; 2013b).

In addition to his regional and global hybrid tough and tender hegemonic masculinity, then, Obama also constructed a global dominating "tough" masculinity in the form of "extrajudicial executions" or legally unauthorized targeted killings through the use of drones. Although Bush also was involved in extrajudicial executions, this practice has increased under Obama. The first drones were flown in Afghanistan in 2001, the USA has increased its arsenal of drones from 167 in 2002 to more than 7,000 today, and Obama has ordered more than five times as many drone strikes as did Bush, primarily in Pakistan, Yemen, and Somalia (Human Rights Watch, 2013).

Drones are used for both surveillance and killing capability. They are approximately 27–30 feet in length and can remain in the air for 24 hours, striking homes, vehicles, and public spaces without warning. Such a presence of drones leads to constant fear, anxiety, and stress among the people on the ground, especially given the fact that they are innocent and thus vulnerably powerless to ensure their own safety. Individuals living in Pakistan, Yemen, and Somalia are resultantly disinclined to participate in a wide variety of community activities, such as funerals and assorted public social gatherings (International Human Rights and Conflict Resolution Clinic, 2012).

According to media accounts, selecting targets for assassination is determined by a group of advisers in the White House under the direction of chief counterterrorism adviser Lisa Monaco, who then presents the names chosen to a weekly White House meeting in which an updated "kill list" is assembled (Dozier, 2012). Obama has placed himself at the top of this secret process, reserving the final say on who should be killed, and he allegedly signs off on every execution in Pakistan, Yemen, and Somalia (Becker and Shane, 2012; Cockburn, 2015). His authorization then allows the CIA and the Joint Special Operations Command of the military to strike the approved "personality" and "signature" targets (Human Rights Clinic, 2012).

Although Obama (2012a) argues that "drones have not caused a huge number of civilian casualties" because "for the most part they have been very precise," the blast from the missile can extend anywhere from 15–20 meters and shrapnel may spread far beyond that (Amnesty International, 2013). And the immediate consequence of a drone strike is not always the death of those targeted but almost always the injury and death of individuals near the strike. A recent study of U.S. drone strikes in Yemen and Pakistan found that such strikes kill on average 28 *unknown* people for every intended target (Gibson, 2014). In these two countries between 2002 and 2014, the report documents 1,147 people killed during attempts to assassinate 41 targeted men: "In Yemen, strikes against just 17 targets accounted for almost half of all confirmed casualties" and "in Pakistan, 221 people, including 103 children, have been killed in attempts to kill four men" (p. 1). Additionally disturbing is the fact that the drone strikes are not as "precise" as Obama claims. Of the seventeen targeted men in Yemen, at least four are still alive and of the four targeted in Pakistan, three are still alive and the fourth died of natural causes.

An example of the above is the case of a drone strike in Pakistan on February 14, 2009, in which the United States targeted Baitullah Mehsud, the leader of the Pakistan Taliban. The strike on that day missed Mehsud, but his eight-year-old son and thirty villagers lost their lives as a result of the strike. Press reports indicate that it would take another *five* strikes before Mehsud actually was assassinated by a U.S. drone and "as many as 164 people lost their lives before Mehsud was eventually killed on 5 August 2009" (Gibson, 2014: 13). This raises an important question: "With each failed attempt to assassinate a man on the Kill List, who filled the body bag in his place? In fact, it is more accurate to say 'body bags': many other lives are sacrificed in the effort to erase a name from the Kill List" (p. 1). This is not surprising as the fired missiles kill in various ways—such as incineration and the crushing of internal organs because of the power of the blast waves—as well as causing disfiguring burns and shrapnel wounds, limb amputations, and vision and hearing loss by those injured (International Human Rights and Conflict Resolution Clinic, 2012). The missiles travel faster than the speed of sound and their victims consequently never hear the missiles that kill or maim them (Cockburn, 2015).

Obama has ordered both "personality" strikes—targeting and executing alleged leaders of terrorist organizations—as well as "signature" strikes, or targeting groups of men who possibly have "defining characteristics" associated with "militant activity or association," but whose identities are unknown (Human Rights Clinic, 2012: 8; Cockburn, 2015). It has never been made public by the White House exactly what the "defining characteristics" actually are, what is meant by "militant activity," and how a drone pilot can determine "militant association" from thousands of miles away. And as this book goes to press it was announced in the media and by Obama that two western hostages—one a U.S. citizen—were killed January 15, 2015, during a "signature" drone strike on an Al Qaida compound in northern Pakistan. Also killed in the attack was a U.S. citizen who was a member of Al Qaida and four days later in a separate "signature" drone strike another U.S. citizen—likewise a member of Al Qaida—was killed (Shane, 2015). These are not the only westerners killed in Obama's drone war—five additional U.S. citizens and thirty-eight total westerners have been killed by drones since first used in 2002 (Woods and Serle, 2015).

It is difficult to gain overall data on strike casualties because the Obama Administration shields the drone program from public accountability, compounded by the obstacles to independent investigation of strikes in the various countries attacked. The best available overall data on drone strikes comes from the Bureau of Investigative Journalism, an independent journalist organization. According to the Bureau's most recent estimates (June 2015):

Pakistan 2004–2015

Total strikes: 418
Total killed: 3,967
Civilians killed: 962
Children killed: 207
Injured: 1,727

Yemen 2002–2015

Total strikes: 117
Total killed: 673
Civilians killed: 97
Children killed: 9
Injured: 217

Somalia 2007–2015

Total strikes: 13
Total killed: 105
Civilians killed: 5
Children killed: 0
Injured: 7

What this data reveals is that more than 27 percent of those killed through drone extrajudicial executions are civilians and children.

This constitutes a global dominating masculinity whereby Obama, serving as judge, jury, and executioner, is ultimately deciding who will live and who will die, he is exercising global power and control over the people of Pakistan, Yemen, and Somalia—Obama is "calling the shots" and "running the show," but he is not legitimating unequal relations between men and women, masculinity and femininity.

REGIONAL AND GLOBAL STRUCTURED ACTION

The combined speeches of both Bush and Obama present a clas-
sic example of how a construct of hegemonic masculinity is constituted regionally and globally through the social process of embodied discursive structured action. Bush's and Obama's
speeches were circulated widely to regional and global audiences
and a villain-victim-hero discursive and relational social structure
was seized upon by both Bush and Obama, who, in turn, reproduced anew this widespread mythical fable—duality of structure
and action materialized as well as congruence between sex and
gender. More specifically, Bush and Obama drew from the villain-victim-hero combined discursive and relational social structure that is grounded historically in a cultural fascination with
stereotypes of the bestial male savage and the captured, raped,
and tormented female. Beginning with the captivity narratives of
the 1600s and 1700s (Kolodny, 1985; Carroll, 2007; Castiglia,
1996; Faludi, 2007), and including the practice of lynching during
post–Civil War Reconstruction (Messerschmidt, 2006), a nation-
alist U.S. culture was in part constructed centering on brutal and
ruthless villains (Native American and African American men),
helpless and innocent captive and abused victims (white Puritan
and planter women), and protecting and rescuing heroes (white
Puritan and planter men). As Susan Jeffords (1991a: 10) points
out, some of the "earliest and most formative popular self-percep-
tions" in the United States "were bound up with the idea that
racial difference constitutes a danger requiring the protection of
victimized women by white men." The captivity and lynching paradigms helped shape and promote a peculiar regional hegemonic
masculine protection and rescue discursive and relational social
structure that became part of U.S. cultural identity (Fitzpatrick,
1991). Not surprisingly, Bush's and Obama's tripartite metaphorical construction of a villain-victim-hero discourse constituted a

contemporary captivity narrative and thus reproduced this discursive and relational social structure in a new way (see also, Jeffords, 1991a; 1991b). And this peculiar regional hegemonic masculinity provided the cultural material for its simultaneous global adoption.

The figure of hero is central both to Western public imagery of the masculine and to Bush's and Obama's embodied discursive structured action. As Antony Whitehead (2005: 413) puts it: "The Hero is replicated in mythology and entertainment *across* social divisions between men, be that through Arthurian legend, Victorian poetry, or American films." Throughout the Western world, the hegemonically masculine hero is extolled culturally and circulated discursively in literature, the mass media, and in politics. For example, from the heroic feature film and TV fantasy icons of Wyatt Earp, the Lone Ranger, and Hopalong Cassidy to James Bond, Dirty Harry, Rambo, Indiana Jones, Superman, and Spiderman, it is understood that these men are the sole individuals with sufficient skills and noble qualities to conquer whatever villain threatens any victim. In these heroic fables, the same story is told consistently: the brave heroic man conquers the diabolical villain, proves his superior masculinity with panache by rescuing and protecting the damsel-in-distress victim, and then takes his well-deserved seat at the pinnacle of the patriarchal status hierarchy (Holt and Thompson, 2004). Bush's and Obama's speechifying, then, drew from this specific discursive and relational social structure and concurrently reproduced these social structures— the duality of structure and action and congruence between sex and gender transpired.

But in addition, Bush's and Obama's speeches reproduced this discursive and relational social structure in a new way by first identifying certain gendered qualities associated with villain, victim, and hero and then placing these gendered qualities in an inferior/superior relationship. For example, both Bush and Obama depict themselves as embodying strength, assertiveness, knowledge, invulnerability, and the ability to protect others as gendered qualities while all "other" people of the world are portrayed as passively dependent, innocent, uninformed, vulnerable, and unable to protect themselves as gendered qualities. Both sets of qualities in Western societies historically and culturally have been associated with men and women respectively, masculinity and femininity respectively, and when these gendered qualities are paired together symbolically in a complementary and subordinate—albeit disembodied—way we have the legitimation of gender inequality through the discursive construction of hegemonic masculinity and emphasized femininity. Congruence between sex and gender then was prevalent.

Both Bush's and Obama's speeches additionally construct a hero-villain masculine relationship that is based on differing unequal gendered qualities attached to each—the hero is civilized, virtuous, just, and peaceful; the villains are uncivilized, cruel, unjust, and violent—and so this pairing signifies an unequal relationship between two different types of masculinities: one hegemonic and one subordinate. The villains are excessively toxic and uncivilized while the heroes are sensibly fair-minded and civilized. Bush's and Obama's gendered qualities were deemed superior in relation to those gender characteristics attached to Saddam Hussein, the Taliban, Al Qaida, and most recently the so-called Islamic State. An overabundance of masculinity symbolically embodied in the villains then actually is represented relationally as a form of masculine inadequacy and deficiency. But in addition, Bush added (and Obama did not) that he would engage in violence *only when necessary* to protect all "civilized" people throughout the world. In this way Bush constructed himself as *the* morally-superior-reluctant-but-critically-necessary fighter and rendered masculine violence as normal, acceptable, and mandatory in especially those situations where "probable" future *lawless* and hypermasculine violence must be suppressed. Given the continued terrorist threat, protective violence became not simply justifiable but imperative—that is, *not* to transgress his explicit and customary masculine interdict against violence would be itself an unacceptable transgression. Constructing himself regionally and globally as the tough *and* tender hybrid *hegemonic masculine heroic protector*, then, Bush solely controlled and neutralized *the* villainous danger to the world. Obama also constructed himself regionally and globally as a tough and tender hybrid *hegemonic masculine heroic protector* but in a different way: Obama emphasized airstrikes and counterterrorism measures as well as humanitarian assistance in counteracting the villainous threat.

In addition to the mythical villain-victim-hero discursive and relational social structure, both Bush and Obama arguably draw from the patriarchal family discursive and relational social structure whereby the heroic masculine heterosexual protector is not a dominating and overpowering presence in the household. Rather, he courageously confronts outside dangers in order to safeguard women and children from harm. This unequal relationship between protector and protected, then, does not constitute submission to a dominating tyrant. Instead, women and children admire their protector and contentedly submit to him in return for the protection that he offers (Young, 2003).

Similarly, in both their embodied communicative structured actions, Bush and Obama adopted from this discursive and relational social structure a contemporary patriarchal position as global heroic hegemonic masculine protectors, instructing all possible victims worldwide to entrust their lives to the two U.S. presidents, in return for which the presidents will do what is necessary to keep the possible victims safe from the villains. Bush and Obama fashioned themselves regionally as *hegemonic masculine heroic protectors* of all U.S. citizens, situating themselves as superior to their subordinate, dependent, and emphasized feminine subjects. Bush and Obama constructed a regional relationship to the U.S. citizenry that is analogous to the masculine heterosexual protector toward his wife and the other members of the patriarchal household, in the sense that his "masculine superiority flows not from acts of repressive domination but from his willingness to risk and sacrifice for others," who in turn both submit to his power and rejoice in his ability to protect them from outside villains (Young, 2003: 9). The hegemonically masculine heterosexual heroic protector then places the protected in a subordinate position of dependence like that of women in the patriarchal household that in turn constructs a gender hegemonic relationship between president and citizen, and hegemonic masculinity intersects here discursively and relationally with heterosexuality.

Bush and Obama likewise forged themselves as global hegemonic protectors by presenting Saddam Hussein's, the Taliban's, Al Qaida's, and the Islamic State's specific brands of toxic metaphorical villainous masculinities as exceptionally dangerous to the world. By resolutely and bravely protecting the people of the world from such terrorists, then, Bush and Obama cast themselves as *the* righteous and thus superior metaphorical heroic protectors. Bush and Obama represented the terrorists as currently "plotting terror" against men, women, and children of the world and, consequently, against innocent, vulnerable, and unsuspecting citizens who were dependent upon Bush's and Obama's focused, steadfast, and unwavering protection to forestall any attack from Saddam Hussein, the Taliban, Al Qaida, and the Islamic State. In contrast to the terrorists' subordinate toxic masculinity, Bush's and Obama's protector hegemonic masculinity constituted a valiant, resolute, and lawful safekeeping of global dependent and feminized citizens against outside aggression. And Bush's and Obama's protector hegemonic masculinities are different from Jessie's protector hegemonic masculinity (see chapter 4) in that the former emphasize defense, security, and safety whereas the latter highlights caring, guidance, and support.

For Bush and Obama all possible victims worldwide were placed in the same structured position: under the direction of each president as sole fatherly protector. In the combined narrative of both sets of speeches, emphasized femininity was disassociated symbolically from the female body as Bush and Obama feminized all possible victims—men, women, and children—through their discursive structured action. Accordingly, worldwide possible victims were subordinated collectively in a gendered relationship to the superior qualities of their masculine protectors. Bush and Obama stressed the dependent and subordinate status of people worldwide as heroically protected by them from the terrorists. People of the world were characterized as emphasized feminine, helpless, innocent, and vulnerable charges wholly in need of protection from the evil, toxic, and subordinate masculine terrorists. Bush's and Obama's discursive structured action denied agency to Saddam Hussein, the Taliban, Al Qaida, and the Islamic State and to the people of the world: the former are "evil" creatures who simply act through bodily impulses rather than through rational and strategic logic; the latter are a collective of "passive dependents" whose fate is determined through the actions of metaphorical toxically masculine villains and hegemonic masculine heroes. Bush and Obama embodied hegemonic masculinity by discursively becoming the sole players granted agency in this tripartite relationship. A global gendered power relationship is socially structured discursively and based on superior/inferior characteristics that legitimated and differentiated unequally hegemonic masculinity from toxic subordinate masculinity and worldwide emphasized feminine men, women, and children. The worldwide citizenry was encouraged to entrust their lives to Bush and Obama, thereby constructing the U.S. presidents as *the* morally superior and culturally exemplary global patriarchal hegemonic masculine individuals who will lead the international effort to protect the world.

In addition to protection, the rescue component of specifically Bush's narrative is likewise drawn from the socially structured discursive fascination with stereotypes of the bestial male savage and the captured, raped, and tormented female. Bush's reproduction of the tripartite metaphorical villain-victim-hero discursive and relational social structure constituted in part a contemporary rescue-from-captivity narrative at the global level. Bush's discursive structured action established a hierarchical gendered relationship between Bush and the people of Iraq by subordinating the vulnerable and innocent emphasized feminine "Oriental" to the strong, invulnerable, and hegemonically masculine "Western" U.S. president. For Bush, Iraqi men were just as dependent upon him (the hero) for rescue from their villainous captor (Saddam Hussein) as were Iraqi women and children. The reality constructed in Bush's discursive structured action was that Iraqi men were utterly incapable of confronting their oppressor and safeguarding "their" women and children from rape, torture, and brutalization, and were, therefore, solely dependent upon Bush rescuing all from the villainous captor. Bush once again therefore dissociated and separated femininity from the female body, he feminized and infantilized Iraqi men by aligning them with women and children, and he thereby constructed them as wholly impotent to confront their captivity. As the hegemonic masculine hero rescuing emphasized feminine and infantile Iraqi men, women, and children from their villainous subordinate masculine captor, then, Bush constructed himself regionally and globally as the *hegemonic masculine heroic rescuer*. The characteristics and attributes associated with Bush and Iraqi men, women, and children assembled discursively an unequal structured gender relationship between the Western Bush and the "Oriental others." A hierarchical power relationship based on superior/inferior embodied gendered characteristics was constructed between rescuer and captive.

Because Saddam Hussein opposed the gender morality Bush represented, he stood clearly outside the world as an enemy of international "civilized" gender relations and as a universal subordinate toxic masculine villain. Bush's communicative social action is a contribution to Edward Said's (1978) notion of "Orientalism," a discourse that posits how the "West" understands the "Orient," and in turn how Westerners understand themselves. In Bush's discourse, the "Oriental Other" is either emphasized feminine and infantile (Iraqi men, women, and children) or barbaric, beastly, and toxically masculine (Saddam Hussein); thus, both "Others" embodied characteristics maintaining an essential gendered inability for self-determination. Bush is discursively constructed as the sole player granted agency in the international arena: the toxic masculine metaphorical villain was a creature of nature that simply acted through bodily impulses rather than rational and strategic logic—and thus must be controlled by Bush. Iraqi men, women, and children likewise were "passive captive things"—the metaphorical victims—whose fate was determined solely by the rescue and continued guidance of Bush. Accordingly, Bush solely embodied the moral, rational, and physically superior global hegemonic masculine qualities requisite to rescue successfully a persecuted and captive population while simultaneously and of necessity presiding over the Iraqi people's progress toward freedom, democracy, and inevitable "civilization."

As global heroic masculine protectors (and rescuer, for Bush) Bush and Obama drew on specifically intersecting discursive and relational social structures in constructing their particular forms of embodied discursive structured actions. Through their speeches, the two U.S. presidents targeted both regional and global audiences in order to "sell" them on their individual virtues and thereby gain support for U.S. military assaults against Iraq and Afghanistan. Owing to their speechifying, Bush and Obama contributed to affirming and possibly stabilizing globally the ascendant position of men over women and Bush and Obama over "all." Their stories of subordinate masculine villains about to attack feminine worldwide potential victims constituted discursively the reason for responding militarily against Iraq and Afghanistan, which, in turn, established Bush and Obama as global hegemonic masculine heroic protectors (and rescuer, for Bush).

The analyses here also supports the notion that *local* hegemonic masculinities may have a certain "family resemblance" to regional and global hegemonic masculinities (see chapter 1). In other words, regional and global hegemonic masculine social structures arguably operate in the localized cultural domain discursively as potential on-hand material to be actualized (or challenged) through practice. For example, in a study of gender hegemony in a U.S. high school, Pascoe (2011) describes a yearly assembly in which senior boys compete to be named the most popular boy in the school by performing skits. The favored skit involved two white boys proving their local hegemonic masculinity by metaphorically *heroically rescuing* "helpless" white girls who were kidnapped and thus became the captive *victims* of a gang of racial minority *villainous* "gangstas." And the localized protective hegemonic masculinity constructed by Jessie (chapter 4) is somewhat similar to—but also very different from—what is being fashioned here by both Bush and Obama regionally and globally.

Although Pascoe's and Jessie's examples demonstrate variable constructions of hegemonic masculinity at the local, regional, and global levels linked by a common core of heroic rescue and/or protection, we should not conclude that there exists exclusively one symbolic model of hegemonic masculinity at all three levels. In fact, as at the local level, there exists a diversity of hegemonic masculinities at the regional and global levels. For example, in her work on hegemonic masculinities and multinational corporations, Juanita Elias (2008) shows how certain qualities of this particular hegemonic masculinity—such as rationality and competition—are built into the culture of multinational corporations, and how such a hegemonic masculinity can be understood only in its *relation* to the qualities attached to the femininity of the women workers in these same corporations: docile and diligent nimble-fingered factory "girls." Although the particular masculine and feminine qualities linked to this particular corporate gender hegemony differ markedly from those gender qualities articulated by both Bush and Obama in their varying heroic hegemonic masculine discursive structured actions, what unites all three of these contrasting forms of hegemonic masculinity is the regional and global *legitimation of a hierarchical relationship between men and women, masculinity and femininity*.

Furthermore, the work of Elias and the content analysis data presented in this chapter supports Connell's (2005; 2009) signature statement on hegemonic masculinity and globalization. Permit me to briefly outline her approach and how the discussion here fits squarely into the notion of a *global gender order*. First, Connell (2005: 72) defines globalization as "the current pattern of world integration via global markets, transnational corporations, and electronic media under the political hegemony of the United States." Second, Connell illuminates how a global gender order is articulated as part of this larger operation of globalization, targeting two basic links currently constituting a global gender order. The first link involves the interaction, interconnection, and interdependence of nation-states and their regional gender orders. As Connell (p. 73) puts it: "The gender patterns resulting from these interactions are the first level of a global gender order. They are [regional] patterns but carry the impress of the forces that make a global society." The second link creates new "spaces" beyond individual nation-states: transnational and multinational corporations (that maintain strong gender divisions of labor and strong masculinist management cultures), the international state (centered on a masculinized character toward diplomacy and war), the international media (consisting of multinational firms that circulate gendered meanings through film, video, music, and news worldwide), and global markets (the increasing reach of capital, commodity, service, and labor markets into individual nation-state economies). The combination of these forms of linkage is "a partially integrated, highly unequal, and turbulent set of gender relations, with global reach but uneven impact"—this now structures the context for considering the construction of local, regional, and global hegemonic masculinities (p. 74). Arguably, Elias' work on multinational corporations and my instant work on the two most recent U.S. presidents are relevant examples of three *differing* types of hegemonic masculinities that accord with the "second link" identified above, and are, therefore, salient components of the "global gender order."

Accordingly, regional and global hegemonic masculinities merge in Bush's and Obama's discursive structured action on how political leaders should behave, and how the global gendered world order should be arranged. In constructing these narratives, then, Bush and Obama imposed a specific discourse on an international conflict, qualifying themselves exclusively as both regional and global hegemonic masculine heroic protectors (and rescuer for Bush). In essence, Bush and Obama constructed these forms of structured action by claiming that they alone spoke with a worldwide masculine voice—representing themselves as *the* paradigmatic masculine model for international gender relations.

In addition, both Bush and Obama engaged or are currently engaging in dominating masculine practices worldwide and thus constructed—for the most part—a behind-the-scenes global dominating presidential masculinity. Because of their international power as leaders of *the* superpower, Bush and Obama have

used that power to determine who worldwide should be subjected to detention, rendition, and torture, and how and who
should be executed extrajudicially. Bush's and Obama's global
power enabled both to set the agenda for how the so-called global
war on terrorism should be addressed. Bush and Obama "called
the shots" and "ran the show," and in the process this permitted
both to embody a global dominating presidential masculinity.

What this chapter alerts us to is how masculine agency within
the institutional setting of the state can be practiced in similar and
differing ways. By contrasting both Bush's and Obama's regional
and global hegemonic masculinities we observe actual *continuity*
between the two presidents: both presidents drew from a victim-
villain-hero intersecting discursive and regional social structure
and in turn constructed regional and global hegemonic masculinities discursively; they reproduced the relational and discursive
structures while simultaneously fashioning behind-the-scenes global dominating masculinities. Although the two U.S. presidents
differed in terms of protector/rescuer (Bush) and protector (Obama), as well as constructing differing types of hybrids, their discursive structured action provided and continues to provide the
rationale, justifications, and the social consensus (throughout the
Western world and Australia and Japan) for the "global war on
terror." To be sure, the regional and global protector hegemonic
masculinities fashioned by Bush and Obama are interwoven with
and an essential element of the perpetual global war on terror—
the latter truly cannot be established and sustained without the
former, as they co-constitute each other. And an interlocking
complex of "protective" social institutions—in the United States
consisting of over 1,200 government bodies working on "counterterrorism," such as the Department of Homeland Security, the
National Security Agency (and its widespread surveillance and
data collection), and the Transportation Security Administration's
"protective" procedures at airports (see Jackson, 2011)—provide

a concrete external "reality" and thus legitimacy of the co-constituted hegemonically masculine war on terror. Finally, through Bush's "detention, rendition, and torture" and Obama's "extrajudicial executions" both presidents *contradicted* and negated their heroic discourses and obscured their alleged alignment with being civilized, virtuous, just, and peaceful.

CONCLUSION

The interview data in chapters 3 and 4 and the content analysis data in chapter 5 yield compelling findings that suggest future research directions for masculinities scholars. Permit me then to conclude this work with a brief summary of the key findings on the three disparate groups of wimps, genderqueers, and presidents and correspondingly provide ten suggestions for prospective and subsequent scholarship on masculinities.

First, Sam, Jerry, Jessie, Morgan, Bush, and Obama drew upon relational and discursive social structures to engage in masculine social action and in turn they reproduced and sometimes changed those social structures through their distinct practices. It would therefore be invaluable for masculinities scholars to investigate further how *duality* between structure and action occurs and how this pertains to masculinities. But additionally it would also be helpful for researchers to investigate when *dualism* between structure and action takes place; that is, when and why individuals distance and separate themselves from, and possibly resist, social structures and how this is related to specific forms of masculine construction. Finally, we need much work on the different types of social structures—for example, relational versus discursive, but also additional social structures—and how such structures impact social action separately as well as how they often intersect and work jointly, but also at times contradictorily.

Second, Sam, Jerry, Jessie, and Morgan constructed sex, gender, and sexuality through specific forms of embodied social practices in specific structural settings. Each of their life stories is constituted by a succession of gender constructions that never reappear—their gender and masculine identities change through time and place. We contextually enact gender anew, even though our sex and sexuality identities may persist unchanged. And this "doing gender" situationally of course remains a much needed scholarly area for research on masculinities. Linked with this is the necessity of exploring when sex is judged to be congruent or incongruent with gender/sexuality by copresent interactants and how this relates to masculinity challenges. During various stages of their life histories, Sam, Jerry, Jessie, and Morgan experienced myriad configurations of congruence and incongruence that impacted their masculine practices, and Bush and Obama constructed congruence discursively. What's more, the mobilization of masculinities by Sam, Jerry, Jessie, Morgan, Bush, and Obama reveal how such masculinities can be manifested in unique ways: Sam wanted to shed his hybridity (because of its association with femininity) whereas Jerry, Jessie, Morgan, Bush, and Obama celebrated and embraced their hybrid masculine constructions. Notwithstanding, early in their lives both Jessie and Morgan completely devalued femininity yet eventually came to adopt femininity as part of their gender identity. Jessie's and Morgan's unique life histories then reveal an ever-changing diversity of hybrid gender orchestrations, culminating in the subsequent hybridization of a genderqueer identity. But an additional interesting aspect of Jessie's and Morgan's hybrid masculinities is how their conception of tomboy masculinity guided their refusal to submit to the attempt by heterosexual boys to subordinate them in terms of gender and sexuality and, therefore, highlights the changing con-

structions of gender for teenage girls and how such changes actually might complicate the reproduction of gender hegemony (see
further Budgeon, 2014). Accordingly, considerable scholarly work
by masculinities researchers on hybrid gender constructions is
needed—especially given its increasing recognized significance
(see Bridges and Pascoe, 2014)—and should be undertaken on
the contrasting ways hybrid masculinities are fashioned by individuals within different contextual milieus throughout their life
course, the similarities and dissimilarities among hybrid masculinities practiced by people assigned as either male or as female at
birth, and how hybridity is related to both hegemonic and nonhegemonic masculinities. And as we have seen through the examples of Bush and Obama, not all masculinities are accomplished
in the way that Sam, Jerry, Jessie, and Morgan tailored their particular masculinities. That is, Bush and Obama engaged in embodied communicative social action and constructed their (hegemonic) masculinities discursively. In other words, through speechifying they associated themselves with the metaphorical hero
and thus established congruence between sex and gender symbolically. It would therefore be extremely helpful for masculinities
researchers to investigate the differing ways individuals construct
masculinities and how congruence and incongruence—as well as
hybridity—are related to those particular constructions. Finally, I
have emphasized in this book the intersection of sex, gender, and
sexuality, yet it is essential that gender scholars appreciate further
the intersectionality of masculinities with such other social dynamics as class, race, ethnicity, age, and nation.

Third, considerable work by masculinities scholars should be
undertaken on reflexivity, or engaging in internal conversations
with oneself about particular social experiences and how individuals decide to respond appropriately. As evidenced herein it is
possible to investigate empirically such reflexivity and the life-
history data clearly demonstrate that Sam, Jerry, Jessie, and Mor-

gan internally mulled over specific interactions and social structures, they considered how particular social circumstances made
them feel, they prioritized what mattered most at specific times,
and they planned and decided how to respond and thus act (see
further Archer, 2012). And such data on reflexivity is essential to
conceptualizing masculine agency and therefore remains a crucial
area for future research. This does not of course deny the fact that
at certain times and in specific situations nonreflexive practicing
of gender may be prevalent (see Martin, 2003; 2006). It would
therefore be advantageous for gender scholars to investigate
when and under what type of social conditions reflexivity and
nonreflexivity impact masculine constructions.

Fourth, scholars writing from a structured action perspective
should also investigate what I have labeled here "supplemental"
constraints and enablers. What the life stories of Sam, Jerry, Jessie, and Morgan reveal is that social action is not exclusively dependent upon social structures but rather at times it is associated
with such supplemental constraints and enablers as intimate conversations and the body. There exists an essential need therefore
for masculinities researchers to examine how these types of interactions inform future social action. A host of supplemental constraints and enablers are daily accessible and one example not
discussed in this book that warrants research attention is the
Internet and social media and how this medium might impact
masculine social action.

Fifth, abundant research is necessary by masculinities scholars
on hegemonic masculinities and how certain unequal and hierarchical gender relations become culturally ascendant and thus
legitimated at the local, regional, and global levels. Included here
are of course research endeavors that examine the differences
among hegemonic masculinities. For example, we have seen in
this book that hegemonic masculinities vary in the significance
and scope of their legitimating influence—the justifying of un-

equal gender relations by localized hegemonic masculinities is limited to the confines of particular institutions, such as schools, whereas regional and global hegemonic masculinities have respectively a society-wide and worldwide legitimating impact. Scholarship on if and to what extent local, regional, and global consent and consequently legitimation actually is consolidated in support of particular hegemonic masculinities continues to be a significant research area. I have also distinguished between "dominating" and "protective" forms of hegemonic masculinities and accordingly differing types of gendered power. The high school popular boys who verbally abused and feminized Sam and Jerry consolidated their hegemonic power through *dominating* aggressive bullying; in contrast, the distinct types of hegemonic masculine power found in the data for Jessie, Bush, and Obama were established through their contrasting forms of benevolent *protection*. And Jessie's particular construct of a localized protective hegemonic masculinity—emphasizing caring, guidance, and support—challenges notions of hegemonic masculinity as exclusively pernicious and noxious. Jessie's practices demonstrate that "positive" forms of hegemonic masculinity do indeed exist (see further Lomas et al., 2015). These are just three examples of differences among hegemonic masculinities and it would be especially valuable to have more research on these and additional divergent forms. And as part of the ongoing research on hegemonic masculinities it is crucial that such explorations examine how hegemonic masculinities are specifically constructed. For example, in this book localized hegemonic masculinities were fashioned through relational material practices that had a discursive legitimating influence, such as the relationship between the dominant in-school bullies who feminized Sam and Jerry as well as the work by Morris (2008; 2012) and Hatfield (2010) discussed in chapter 1. Regional and global hegemonic masculinities, however, were constructed through discursive practices—such as the speeches of

Bush and Obama as well as the rap albums analyzed by Weitzer and Kubrin (2009) and summarized in chapter 1—that concurrently constituted unequal gender relations linguistically, metaphorically, and thus symbolically. It would be very useful for future research by masculinities scholars to address how hegemonic masculinities are accomplished differently and how their ascendancy is embedded (and often camouflaged) in a diversity of social structures, such as the informal relations of "cliques" in secondary schools and the discursive villain-victim-hero narrative. Arguably, what the life history and content analysis evidence reveals is the omnipresent nature of unequal gender relations— from the local to the regional to the global—and how such pervasiveness often is concealed, not readily apparent, and thus has a somewhat disguised yet overwhelming legitimating influence. Finally, there is an essential need for in-depth research on how globalization impacts regional and local hegemonic masculinities around the world, how hegemonic masculinities differ in terms of the two basic links constituting the global gender order discussed in chapter 5, and how hegemonic masculinities are constructed in periphery (see the studies by Groes-Green [2009] and Broughton [2008] discussed in chapter 1) and postcolonial societies (see further Connell, 2015). Indeed, are theoretical frameworks like structured action theory, as gender paradigms established within the Global North, applicable to the conceptualization of gender relations in the Global South?

Sixth, it is vital that masculinities scholars research the various forms of nonhegemonic masculinities—or those masculinities that do not legitimate gender inequality—in specific social settings. For example, some nonhegemonic masculinities are complicit with hegemonic masculinities (they construct unequal gender relations) yet they are not culturally ascendant and accordingly do not legitimate gender inequality, such as Sam's dominating form of masculinity constructed through sexual violence. Other nonhegemonic masculinities are embedded in hegemonically masculine relations, such as Jessie's subordinate tomboy masculinity, while still other nonhegemonic masculinities include those developed through resistance to hegemonic and dominant masculinities, such as Jerry's positive masculinity that supports equality in gender relations, and are subsequently practiced entirely outside gender hegemonic relations (for example, in Jerry's "laidback" group). We clearly need much work on such positive masculinities as well as the varying forms of gender relations in which they flourish. The differing global dominating masculinities by Bush and Obama are likewise nonhegemonic because they do not legitimate gender inequality and are as well constructed external to regional and global gender hegemonic relations. Finally, "individualized" forms of masculinity are nonhegemonic—such as the "adventurer" masculinity reported by Broughton (2008) and discussed in chapter 1 as well as Morgan's stealth masculinity—because they likewise do not legitimate gender inequality. Clearly, then, it is imperative for masculinities scholars to examine the differing forms of nonhegemonic masculinities and how they relate to hegemonic masculinities at the local, regional, and global levels.

Seventh, as the life stories of Jessie and Morgan demonstrate, masculinity is not determined biologically and thus not exclusively coupled with people assigned male at birth. And this fact surely should lead masculinities scholars to identify and examine possible masculinities constructed by those assigned female at birth as well as those related to the incongruence between sex and masculinity. As further suggested in the case studies of Jessie and Morgan masculinity under certain social conditions may become the primary foundation of one's identity while sex is then transformed into the qualifier. The coherence of one's initial fundamental sex and gender project may be altered whereby *masculinity* becomes primary and "real" and *sex* transmuted into epiphenomenon. We therefore need much more work on when and how masculinity becomes the primary mode in which one relates to the world as well as when femininity becomes the principal foundation of one's identity for people assigned male at birth.

Eighth, there is critical demand for in-depth research on the body and how it both constrains and enables masculine and sexual agency. The life-history data in this book clearly demonstrates the significance of the body to Sam's, Jerry's, Jessie's, and Morgan's changing gender and masculine constructions. All four experienced bodily contradictions in terms of the relationship between sex (body) and gender (masculinity), yet Jessie's and Morgan's bodies took on an added dimension through the sexed meanings of certain bodily developments (for example, breasts and menstruation) as well as the fact that culturally their bodies were expected to be congruent with femininity, not masculinity. Jessie's and Morgan's life stories reveal that girls and women can indeed construct masculinities but there often exists a degree of bodily anxiety in doing so, and their experiences were similar but also very different (see further Connell, 2012). As Morgan's life story in particular demonstrates, the body is essential to masculine constructions in terms of the "two and only two sexes" discursive structure and its accompanying assertion that "men have penises and women do not"—genitalia is significant for one's sex, gender, and sexual attribution. Bodies and their visible parts impact our recurring reflexive self-attributions and thus an identity as masculine both socially and sexually. In nonsexual social situations when Morgan was a "stealth dude" there existed congruence between sex and gender and he easily "passed" as a man yet when in sexual social situations with certain straight women incongruence between sex and gender occurred, leading Morgan to question his maleness (see further Schilt and Windsor, 2014; Westbrook and Schilt, 2014). For Morgan, then, masculinity in certain sexual situations was experienced as a disembodied phenomenon that impacted future practice. And of course the discursive constructions of regional and global hegemonic masculinities by Bush and Obama are completely disembodied as no material bodies actually exist—that is, outside the bodies of Bush and Obama situated behind the microphones and podiums—but rather simply are linguistically and symbolically represented. Considerable work therefore must be undertaken by masculinities scholars on how the ever-changing body is related to the social construction of maleness, masculinity, and sexuality; how the body under specific social situations impacts masculine construction; and how masculinity can be experienced *and* constructed as a disembodied event.

Ninth, the life-history data also reveal further important information regarding the relationship between sexuality and masculine constructions. Sam, Jerry, Jessie, and Morgan initially affixed a heterosexual project to their fundamental sex and gender projects that were governed primarily by interactions at school. Nevertheless, each of these four throughout their individual life course developed unique forms of sexual interaction that were significant to their masculinity constructions, such as sexual violence, celibacy, resistance to heterosexuality, and same-sex and queer relations. And the regional and global hegemonic masculinities by Bush and Obama were constituted discursively through notions of the heterosexual patriarchal family and its heroic masculine protector. Accordingly, it is critical that masculinities scholars thoroughly research the relationship among the diversity of sexualities and how such sexualities may relate to masculinities differently.

Finally, there is an essential need for in-depth research by masculinities scholars that investigates when and how people orchestrate *both* masculinity and femininity or *neither* masculinity nor femininity. The case studies of both Jessie and Morgan are uniquely captivating in the sense that their eventual particular genderqueer constructions represent examples of what Haywood and Mac an Ghaill (2012; 2013) recently labeled "post-masculinities," in the sense of not being exclusively masculine but rather masculinity is merely a specific part of their overall gender construction and not its *sole* defining characteristic. It therefore would be beneficial for masculinities scholars to research genderqueer and other transmasculine identities whereby masculinity plays a partial rather than *the* central role in the social construction of gender.

REFERENCES

Altheide, D. 1996. *Qualitative Media Analysis.* Thousand Oaks, CA: Sage.

Amnesty International. 2013. *"Will I Be Next?" US Drone Strikes in Pakistan.* London: Amnesty International.

Archer, M. S. 2003. *Structure, Agency, and the Internal Conversation.* New York: Cambridge University Press.

———. 2007. *Making Our Way through the World: Human Reflexivity and Social Mobility.* New York: Cambridge University Press.

———. 2012. *The Reflexive Imperative in Late Modernity.* New York: Cambridge University Press.

Beasley, C. 2008. "Rethinking Hegemonic Masculinity in a Globalizing World." *Men and Masculinities* 11 (1): 86–103.

———. 2013. "Rethinking Hegemonic Masculinity in Transnational Context." In J. Hearn, M. Blagojevic, and K. Harrison, eds. *Rethinking Transnational Men: Beyond, Between, and Within Nations,* 29–44. New York: Routledge.

Becker, J., and S. Shane. May 29, 2012. "Secret 'Kill List' Proves a Test of Obama's Principles and Will." *The New York Times.*

Berg, B. 1998. *Qualitative Research Methods for the Social Sciences.* Boston: Allyn & Bacon.

Bridges, T., and C. J. Pascoe. 2014. "Hybrid Masculinities: New Directions in the Sociology of Men and Masculinities." *Sociology Compass* 8 (3): 246–258.

Broughton, C. 2008. "Migration as Engendered Practice: Mexican Men, Masculinity, and Northward Migration." *Gender & Society* 22 (5): 568–589.

Budgeon, S. 2014. "The Dynamics of Gender Hegemony: Femininities, Masculinities, and Social Change." *Sociology* 48 (2): 317–334.

Bureau of Investigative Journalism. 2015. "Casualty Estimates." http://www.thebureauinvestigates.com.

Bush, G. W. 2010. *Decision Points.* New York: Crown.

Carroll, L. 2007. *Rhetorical Drag: Gender Impersonation, Captivity, and the Writing of History.* Kent, OH: Kent State University Press.

Castiglia, C. 1996. *Bound and Determined: Captivity, Culture-Crossing, and White Womanhood from Mary Rowlandson to Patty Hearst.* Chicago: University of Chicago Press.

Cealey Harrison, W. 2006. "The Shadow and the Substance: The Sex/Gender Debate." In K. Davis, M. Evans, and J. Lorber, eds. *Handbook of Gender and Women's Studies*, 35–52. Thousand Oaks, CA: Sage.

Cockburn, A. 2015. *Kill Chain: The Rise of the High-Tech Assassins.* New York: Henry Holt and Company.

Cole, D. 2015. "Torture: No One Said No." *The New York Review of Books.* March 5. http://www.nybooks.com.

Committee on Armed Services. 2008. *Inquiry into the Treatment of Detainees in US Custody.* Washington, DC: United States Senate.

Connell, R. 1987. *Gender and Power.* Sydney: Allen and Unwin.

———. 1995. *Masculinities.* Cambridge: Polity Press.

———. 1998. "Making Gendered People: Bodies, Identities, Sexualities." In M. M. Ferree, J. Lorber, and B. B. Hess, eds. *Revisioning Gender*, 449–471. Thousand Oaks, CA: Sage.

———. 2000. *The Men and the Boys.* Sydney: Allen and Unwin.

———. 2005. "Globalization, Imperialism, and Masculinities." In M. S. Kimmel, J. Hearn, and R. Connell, eds., *Handbook of Studies on Men & Masculinities.* Thousand Oaks, CA: Sage.

———. 2007. *Southern Theory.* Cambridge, UK: Polity.

———. 2008. "A Thousand Miles from Kind: Men, Masculinities, and Modern Institutions." *The Journal of Men's Studies* 16 (3): 237–252.

———. 2009. *Gender.* Second edition. Cambridge: Polity Press.

———. 2012. "Transsexual Women and Feminist Thought: Toward New Understanding and New Politics." *Signs: Journal of Women in Culture and Society* 37 (4): 857–881.

———. 2015. "Meeting at the Edge of Fear: Theory on a World Scale." *Feminist Theory* 16 (1): 49–66.

Connell, R., and J. W. Messerschmidt. 2005. "Hegemonic Masculinity: Rethinking the Concept." *Gender & Society* 19 (6): 829–859.

Crenshaw, K. 1991. "Mapping the Margins: Intersectionality, Identity Politics, and Violence against Women of Color." *Stanford Law Review* 43:1241–1299.

Crossley, N. 1995. "Body Techniques, Agency and Intercorporeality: On Goffman's *Relations in Public.*" *Sociology* 29 (1): 133–149.

———. 2001. *The Social Body: Habit, Identity, and Desire.* Thousand Oaks, CA: Sage.

Davis, K. 2008. "Intersectionality as Buzzword: A Sociology of Science Perspective On What Makes a Feminist Theory Successful." *Feminist Theory* 9 (1): 67–85.

Deutsch, F. 1999. *Halving It All.* Cambridge, MA: Harvard University Press.

Dozier, K. May 21, 2012. "Who Will Drones Target? Who in the US Will Decide?" http://www.salon.com.

Duncanson, C. 2009. "Forces for Good? Narratives of Military Masculinity as Peacekeeping Operations." *International Feminist Journal of Politics* 11 (1): 63–80.

Elias, J. 2008. "Hegemonic Masculinities, the Multinational Corporation, and the Developmental State: Constructing Gender in 'Progressive' Firms." *Men and Masculinities* 10 (4): 405–421.

Elias, J., and C. Beasley. 2009. "Hegemonic Masculinity and Globalization: 'Transnational Business Masculinities' and Beyond." *Globalization* 6 (2): 281–296.

Faludi, S. 2007. *The Terror Dream: Fear and Fantasy in Post-9/11 America*. New York: Metropolitan Books.

Fitzpatrick, T. 1991. "The Figure of Captivity: The Cultural Work of the Puritan Captivity Narrative." *American Literary History* 3 (1): 1–26.

Foucault, M. 1972. *The Archeology of Knowledge*. Translated by A. M. Sheridan Smith. New York: Harper & Row.

———. 1980. *Herculine Barbin*. New York: Vintage.

Gage, E. A. 2008. "Gender Attitudes and Sexual Behaviors: Comparing Center and Marginal Athletes and Nonathletes in a Collegiate Setting." *Violence against Women* 14 (9): 1014–1032.

Gibson, J. 2014. *You Never Die Twice: Multiple Kills in the US Drone Program*. New York: Reprieve US.

Giddens, A. 1976. *New Rules of Sociological Method: A Positive Critique of Interpretive Sociologies*. New York: Basic Books.

———. 1984. *The Constitution of Society*. Berkeley: University of California Press.

———. 1991. *Modernity and Self-Identity*. Stanford, CA: Stanford University Press.

Goffman, E. 1963. *Behavior in Public Places*. New York: Free Press.

———. 1968. *Stigma*. Englewood Cliffs, NJ: Prentice Hall.

———. 1972. *Relations in Public*. New York: Harper & Row.

———. 1979. *Gender Advertisements*. New York: Harper & Row.

Groes-Green, C. 2009. "Hegemonic and Subordinated Masculinities: Class, Violence and Sexual Performance among Young Mozambican Men." *Nordic Journal of African Studies* 18 (4): 286–304.

Hatfield, E. F. 2010. "'What It Means to Be a Man': Examining Hegemonic Masculinity in *Two and a Half Men*." *Communication, Culture & Critique* 3:526–548.

Haywood, C., and M. Mac an Ghaill. 2012. "'What's Next for Masculinity?' Reflexive Directions for Theory and Research on Masculinity and Education." *Gender and Education* 24 (6): 577–592.

———. 2013. *Education and Masculinities: Social, Cultural and Global Transformations*. New York: Routledge.

Hearn, J., M. Blagojevic, and K. Harrison, eds. 2013. *Rethinking Transnational Men: Beyond, Between, and Within Nations*. New York: Routledge.

Hollander, J. A. 2013. "'I Demand More of People': Accountability, Interaction, and Gender Change." *Gender & Society* 27 (1): 5–29.

Holstein, J. A., and J. F. Gubrium. 1995. *The Active Interview*. Thousand Oaks, CA: Sage.

Holt, D. B., and C. J. Thompson. 2004. "Man-of-Action Heroes: The Pursuit of Heroic Masculinity in Everyday Consumption." *Journal of Consumer Research* 31:425–440.

Holtzman, E. 2012. *Cheating Justice*. Boston: Beacon Press.

Human Rights Clinic (Columbia Law School). 2012. *The Civilian Impact of Drones: Unexamined Costs, Unanswered Questions*. Washington, DC: Center for Civilians in Conflict.

Human Rights Watch. 2011. *Getting Away with Torture: The Bush Administration and Mistreatment of Detainees*. New York: Human Rights Watch.

———. 2013. *"Between a Drone and Al-Qaida": The Civilian Cost of US Targeted Killings in Yemen*. New York: Human Rights Watch.

International Human Rights and Conflict Resolution Clinic (Stanford Law School) and Global Justice Clinic (NYU School of Law). 2012. *Living under Drones: Death, Injury, and Trauma to Civilians from US Drone Practices in Pakistan*. http://livingunderdrones.org.

Irvine, L., and J. Vermilya. 2010. "Gender Work in a Feminized Profession: The Case of Veterinary Medicine." *Gender & Society* 24 (1): 56–82.

Jackson, R. 2011. "Culture, Identity and Hegemony: Continuity and (the Lack of) Change in US Counterterrorism Policy from Bush to Obama." *International Politics* 48 (2/3): 390–411.

Jackson, S. 2007. "The Sexual Self in Late Modernity." In M. Kimmel, ed., *The Sexual Self*, 3–15. Nashville, TN: Vanderbilt University Press.

Jackson, S., and S. Scott. 2010. *Theorizing Sexuality*. New York: McGraw-Hill.

Jeffords, S. 1991a. "Protection Racket." *The Women's Review of Books* 8 (10–11): 10.

———. 1991b. "Rape and the New World Order." *Cultural Critique* 19 (Autumn): 203–215.

Jurik, N., and C. Siemsen. 2009. "'Doing Gender' as Canon or Agenda: A Symposium on West and Zimmerman." *Gender & Society* 23 (1): 72–75.

Kessler, S., and W. McKenna. 1978. *Gender: An Ethnomethodological Approach*. New York: John Wiley.

Kitzinger, C. 2005. "'Speaking as a Heterosexual': (How) Does Sexuality Matter for Talk-in-Interaction?" *Research on Language and Social Interaction* 38 (3): 221–265.

Kolodny, A. 1985. *The Land Before Her: Fantasy and Experience of the American Frontiers, 1630–1860*. Chapel Hill, NC: University of North Carolina Press.

Laqueur, T. 1990. *Making Sex: Body and Gender from the Greeks to Freud*. Cambridge, MA: Harvard University Press.

Light, R. 2007. "Re-Examining Hegemonic Masculinity in High School Rugby: The Body, Compliance and Resistance." *Quest* 59:323–338.

Logan, T. D. 2010. "Personal Characteristics, Sexual Behaviors, and Male Sex Work: A Quantitative Approach." *American Sociological Review* 75 (5): 679–704.

Lomas, T., T. Cartwright, T. Edginton, and D. Ridge. 2015. "New Ways of Being a Man: 'Positive' Hegemonic Masculinity in Mediation-based Communities of Practice." *Men and Masculinities.* Published online March 23.

Lorber, J. 2005. *Breaking the Bowls: Degendering and Feminist Change.* New York: Norton.

Martin, P. Y. 1998. "Why Can't a Man Be More Like a Woman? Reflections on Connell's Masculinities." *Gender & Society* 12 (4): 472–474.

———. 2003. "'Said and Done' Versus 'Saying and Doing': Gendering Practices, Practicing Gender at Work." *Gender and Society* 17 (3): 342–366.

———. 2006. "Practicing Gender at Work: Further Thoughts on Reflexivity." *Gender, Work and Organization* 13 (3): 254–276.

McCormack, M. 2011. "Hierarchy without Hegemony: Locating Boys in an Inclusive School Setting." *Sociological Perspectives* 54 (1): 83–101.

McCoy, A. 2006. *A Question of Torture: CIA Interrogation, from the Cold War to the War on Terror.* New York: Metropolitan Books.

Messerschmidt, J. W. 1993. *Masculinities and Crime: Critique and Reconceptualization of Theory.* Lanham, MD: Rowman & Littlefield.

———. 1997. *Crime as Structured Action: Gender, Race, Class, and Crime in the Making.* Thousand Oaks, CA: Sage Publications.

———. 2000. *Nine Lives: Adolescent Masculinities, the Body, and Violence.* Boulder, CO: Westview Press.

———. 2004. *Flesh & Blood: Adolescent Gender Diversity and Violence.* Lanham, MD: Rowman & Littlefield.

———. 2006. "'We Must Protect Our Southern Women': On Whiteness, Masculinities, and Lynching." In M. Bosworth and J. Flavin, eds., *Race, Gender, and Punishment: From Colonialism to the War on Terror,* 77–94. New Brunswick, NJ: Rutgers University Press.

———. 2008. "And Now, the Rest of the Story . . ." *Men and Masculinities* 11 (1): 104–108.

———. 2010. *Hegemonic Masculinities and Camouflaged Politics: Unmasking the Bush Dynasty and Its War against Iraq.* Boulder, CO: Paradigm Publishers.

———. 2012. *Gender, Heterosexuality, and Youth Violence: The Struggle for Recognition.* Lanham, MD: Rowman & Littlefield.

———. 2014. *Crime as Structured Action: Doing Masculinities, Race, Class, Sexuality, and Crime.* Second edition. Lanham, MD: Rowman & Littlefield.

Morgan, D. 1992. *Discovering Men.* New York: Routledge.

Morris, E. W. 2008. "'Rednecks,' 'Rutters,' and 'Rithmetic: Social Class, Masculinity, and Schooling in a Rural Context." *Gender & Society* 22 (6): 728–751.

———. 2012. *Learning the Hard Way: Masculinity, Place, and the Gender Gap in Education.* New Brunswick, NJ: Rutgers University Press.

Mouzelis, N. P. 2008. *Modern and Postmodern Social Theorizing: Bridging the Divide*. New York: Cambridge University Press.

Open Society Foundations. 2013. *Globalizing Torture: CIA Secret Detention and Extraordinary Rendition*. New York: Open Society Foundations.

Paechter, Carrie. 2006. "Masculine Femininities/Feminine Masculinities: Power, Identities, and Gender." *Gender and Education* 18 (3): 253–263.

Pascoe, C. J. 2011. *Dude, You're a Fag: Masculinity and Sexuality in High School*. Second edition. Berkeley, CA: University of California Press.

Patton, M. Q. 1990. *Qualitative Evaluation and Research Methods*. Newbury Park, CA: Sage.

Peterson, A. 2011. "The 'Long Winding Road' to Adulthood: A Risk-Filled Journey for Young People in Stockholm's Marginalized Periphery." *Young* 19 (3): 271–289.

Ruspini, E., J. Hearn, B. Pease, and K. Pringle, eds. 2011. *Men and Masculinities around the World: Transforming Men's Practices*. New York: Palgrave.

Said, E. W. 1978. *Orientalism*. New York: Pantheon.

Sands, P. 2008. *Torture Team: Rumsfeld's Memo and the Betrayal of American Values*. New York: Palgrave.

Sartre, J. P. 1956. *Being and Nothingness*. New York: Washington Square Press.

Schilt, K., and E. Windsor. 2014. "The Sexual Habitus of Transgender Men: Negotiating Sexuality through Gender." *Journal of Homosexuality* 61: 732–748.

Schippers, M. 2007. "Recovering the Feminine Other: Masculinity, Femininity, and Gender Hegemony." *Theory and Society* 36 (1): 85–102.

Seidman, S. 2010. *The Social Construction of Sexuality*. Second edition. New York: Norton.

Senate Select Committee on Intelligence. 2014. *Committee Study of the Central Intelligence Agency's Detention and Interrogation Program: Executive Summary*. http://www.intelligence.senate.gov/study2014/sscistudy1.pdf.

Shane, S. 2015. "Ghosts in the Cross Hairs: Drone Strikes Reveal Uncomfortable Truth: U.S. Is Often Unsure about Who Will Die." *The New York Times*. April 24: A1, A14.

Smith, J., A. Braunack-Mayer, G. Wittert, and M. Warin. 2007. "'I've been independent for so damn long!': Independence, Masculinity and Aging in a Help Seeking Context." *Journal of Aging Studies* 21:325–335.

Talbot, K., and M. Quayle. 2010. "The Perils of Being a Nice Guy: Contextual Variation in Five Young Women's Constructions of Acceptable Hegemonic and Alternative Masculinities." *Men and Masculinities* 13 (2): 255–278.

Weitzer, R., and C. E. Kubrin. 2009. "Misogyny in Rap Music: A Content Analysis of Prevalence and Meanings." *Men and Masculinities* 12 (1): 3–29.

West, C., and S. Fenstermaker. 1995. "Doing Difference." *Gender and Society* 9:8–37.

West, C., and D. Zimmerman. 1987. "Doing Gender." *Gender & Society* 1 (2): 125–151.

Westbrook, L., and K. Schilt. 2014. "Doing Gender, Determining Gender: Transgender People, Gender Panics, and the Maintenance of the Sex/Gender/Sexuality System." *Gender & Society* 28 (1): 32–57.

Whitehead, A. 2005. "Man to Man Violence: How Masculinity May Work as a Dynamic Risk Factor." *The Howard Journal* 44 (4): 411–422.

Wickes, R., and M. Emmison. 2007. "They Are All 'Doing Gender' but Are They All Passing? A Case Study of the Appropriation of a Sociological Concept." *The Sociological Review* 55 (2): 311–330.

Wilkerson, L. 2009. "The Truth about Richard Bruce Cheney." *The Washington Note*. May 13: 1–21.

———. 2014. "Ex-Bush Official: U.S. Tortured Prisoners to Produce False Intel That Built Case for Iraq War." *Democracy Now!* December 23. http://www.democracynow.org.

Yeon Choo, H., and M. M. Ferree, 2010. "Practicing Intersectionality in Sociological Research: A Critical Analysis of Inclusions, Interactions, and Institutions in the Study of Inequalities." *Sociological Theory* 28 (2): 129–149.

Young, I. M. 1990. *Throwing Like a Girl and Other Essays in Feminist Philosophy and Social Theory*. Bloomington: Indiana University Press.

———. 2003. "The Logic of Masculinist Protection: Reflections on the Current Security State." *Signs* 29 (1): 1–25.

FORMER US PRESIDENT GEORGE W. BUSH SPEECHES

2002a. "Address Before a Joint Session of the Congress on the State of the Union," January 29.

2002b. "Remarks on the Six-Month Anniversary of the September 11th Attacks," March 11.

2002c. "Remarks Announcing Bipartisan Agreement on a Joint Resolution to Authorize the Use of United States Armed Forces against Iraq," October 2.

2002d. "Address to the United Nations General Assembly in New York City," September 12.

2002e. "Address to the Nation on Iraq from Cincinnati, Ohio," October 7.

2002f. "Remarks on Signing the Authorization for Use of Military Force against Iraq Resolution of 2002," October 16.

2002g. "Remarks on the Passage of a United Nations Security Council Resolution on Iraq," November 8.

2002h. "The President's Radio Address," January 26.

2002i. "The President's Radio Address," November 9.

2003a. "Remarks on the Iraqi Regime's Noncompliance with United Nations Resolutions," February 6.

2003b. "Address to the Nation on Iraq," March 17.

2003c. "Address to the Nation on Iraq," March 19.

PRESIDENT BARACK OBAMA SPEECHES

2009a. "Remarks on United States Military and Diplomatic Strategies for Afghanistan and Pakistan," March 27.

2009b. "Remarks at a Town Hall Meeting and a Question-and-Answer Session in Strasbourg, France," April 3.

2009c. "Address to the Nation at the United States Military Academy at West Point, New York," December 1.

2009d. "Inaugural Address," January 20.

2009e. "Letter to the Speaker of the House of Representatives Transmitting a Supplemental Appropriations Request for Ongoing Military, Diplomatic, And Intelligence Operations," April 9.

2009f. "Remarks in Cairo," June 4.

2009g. "Remarks at the National Defense University," March 12.

2009h. "The President's News Conference in Strasbourg, France," April 4.

2009i. "Remarks at a Memorial Service at Fort Hood, Texas," November 10.

2009j. "Remarks at the Central Intelligence Agency in Langley, Virginia," April 20.

2009k. "Address Before a Joint Session of Congress," February 24.

2009l. "Remarks Following a Meeting with Defense Secretary Robert M. Gates and the Joint Chiefs of Staff in Arlington, Virginia," January 28.

2009m. "The President's News Conference in Pittsburgh, Pennsylvania," September 25.

2009n. "Remarks on Improving Homeland Security in Kaneohe, Hawaii," December 28.

2010a. "Remarks on Improving Homeland Security," January 7.

2010b. "Remarks to United States and Coalition Troops at Bagram Air Base, Afghanistan," March 28.

2010c. "Remarks Following a Meeting on Improving Homeland Security," January 5.

2010d. "Remarks on the Resignation of General Stanley A. McChrystal as Commander of the NATO International Security Assistance Force in Afghanistan," June 23.

2010e. "The President's News Conference with President Hamid Karzai of Afghanistan," May 12.

2010f. "Remarks at the United States–India Strategic Dialogue Reception," June 3.

2011a. "Remarks on the Death of Al Qaida Terrorist Organization Leader Osama bin Laden," May 1.

2011b. "Statement on the 10th Anniversary of United States Personnel in Afghanistan," October 7.

2012. "Address Before a Joint Session of Congress on the State of the Union," January 24.

2013a. "The President's News Conference with President Hamid Karzai of Afghanistan," January 11.

2013b. "Remarks at National Defense University," May 23.

2014. "Address to the Nation on United States Strategy to Combat the Islamic State of Iraq and the Levant Terrorist Organization," September 10.

INDEX

sports participation, 17–18, 93, 121–122, 125
stealth masculinity, 131–139
structured action theory, 2, 6, 37, 46–63, 184; and Bush and Obama, 155, 167–178; and Jerry, 92
subordinate masculinity, 13, 55, 66–67, 146, 172–175

Talbot, Kirsten, 20, 32
Taliban, 146, 157–162, 169–172
tomboy masculinity, 99–100, 101–104, 114, 120–122
torture, secret detention, and extraordinary rendition, 147, 152–156, 178
toxic and hypermasculinity, 18, 147, 149, 159–160, 169–174
transmasculinity, 112–116, 130–141, 143, 189
Transportation Security Administration, 178
Two and a Half Men, 14–15

vagina, 38, 53, 117, 143
Vermilya, Jenny, 21
veterinary medicine study, 21

villain-victim-hero narrative and social structure, 146, 157, 167, 170, 173, 186
violence and nonviolence, 2, 13, 18, 27, 51, 167–168, 186, 189; and Bush, 147–148, 151, 169; and Jerry, 81, 84–89, 92, 96; and Morgan, 120; and Obama, 158–160, 162, 169; and Sam, 65, 67, 70, 75–77

war on terror, 145–147, 150, 157–158, 178
waterboarding, 153, 155. *See also* torture, secret detention, and extraordinary rendition
weapons of mass destruction, 146, 147–148, 150
Weitzer, Ronald, 13, 32, 184
Whitehead, Antony, 168
Wilkerson, Lawrence, 153
wimps, 55–56, 69–71, 87
World Bank, 25

Young, Iris Marion, 57, 171

ze and zir, 142
Zubaydah, Abu, 153

ABOUT THE AUTHOR

James W. Messerschmidt is professor of sociology and chair of the criminology department at the University of Southern Maine, where he also teaches in the women's and gender studies program. He is the author or coauthor of a number of books, including *Masculinities and Crime* and *Gender, Heterosexuality, and Youth Violence*.